BY PEN AND PULPIT

Canon P.A. Sheehan (1852-1913)
Courtesy Denis Madigan, Doneraile

BY PEN AND PULPIT

THE LIFE AND TIMES
OF THE AUTHOR
CANON SHEEHAN

- by -

MICHAEL BARRY

Saturn Books, Fermoy, Co. Cork.

By the same author:

No Flowers By Request & Other Stories.
Poems For Your Pleasure.
The Romance of Sarah Curran.
An Affair of Honour (Irish Duels & Duelists).
The Story of Cork Airport.
The International Aviation Quiz Book.

Printed by Litho Press Co., Midleton, Co. Cork.

Acknowledgements:

I wish to thank very sincerely **AER RIANTA** Cork Airport for their generous support.

My sincere thanks also to the following for their kind assistance during my research:

Michael Shine, Doneraile; The Public Record Office, Dublin; The Staffs of the National Library, the Cork County & City Libraries and the Fermoy County Library; C. Gordon Vaughn, MD, St. Paul's, Minnesota; Mrs. Mary O'Keeffe, Derryvillane, Mitchelstown; Presentation Convent, Doneraile; Convent of Mercy, Mallow; Walter McGrath, Cork; Rev. T. Sheehan (former Bishop's Sec.); Rev. Fr. D. O'Brien, Stanley, Co. Durham; Rev. Fr. Francis A. Carbine, Philadelphia; The Archivist, St. Charles Borromeo Seminary, Overbrook, Philadelphia; Michael Bott, Archivist, University of Reading; Irish Govt. Publications Office; Miss Deirdre Sheehan, Mallow Heritage Centre; The North Cork Writers' Committee, Doneraile.

My thanks and appreciation also to the publishers Longman Group UK. Ltd., for permission to quote their sales figures in Ireland of the Canon Sheehan books they published. Similarly to Michael Gill of Gill & Macmillan regarding the sales figures of Canon Sheehan's first book *Geoffrey Austin, Student,* published by M.H. Gill & Son and also to An Gum for the sales figures of the books by Canon Sheehan translated into Irish.

I would also like to acknowledge the assistance of the late Mother Benignus of Presentation Convent, Doneraile who gave me her reminiscences of Canon Sheehan and also John O'Toole, Graigue, Shanballymore who did likewise.

A special acknowledgement for the assistance of the late Miss Sheila Power, Ballywalter, Shanballymore who kindly put me in touch with Fr. Carbine of Philadelphia regarding the Heuser Papers.

The title of this book *"By Pen and Pulpit"* was suggested by my good friend Edward Garner.

Michael Barry

INTRODUCTION

In the early decades of this century Canon Sheehan was a household name throughout Ireland and very widely known abroad. There were few homes where some if not all of his many books such as *My New Curate, The Blindness of Dr. Gray, Glenanaar etc.* were not to be found. Today he is almost forgotten, except perhaps in his native Mallow and in Doneraile where he wrote all his books and where he is buried.

The purpose of this book is twofold; firstly to bring to the notice of this generation the life and works of a much loved Irish priest who became an internationally acclaimed author; secondly I feel it is a worthwhile exercise almost eighty years after his death to look at this man and the part he played in the Ireland of his time (1852-1913) and about which he wrote with sympathy.

To aid me in my research, I was fortunate in getting access to correspondence and documents re Canon Sheehan in the papers of Herman J. Heuser, D.D. housed in the archives of St. Charles Borromeo Seminary, Overbrook, Philadelphia. Much of this hitherto unpublished material gives details of the Canon's successful land-ownership negotiations on behalf of the Doneraile tenant-farmers following the passing of the Wyndham Land Act of 1903. There is considerable data too on the controversy which went on for some years between Mallow and Doneraile as to where a national monument to Canon Sheehan should be sited. There is the Holmes-Sheehan correspondence (1903-1913) which tells us much about the Doneraile pastor and his thinking in letters to the famed United States lawyer Justice Oliver Wendell Holmes Jnr.

I have included too the rather bizarre incident in Mallow in 1878 during the Canon's first curacy there when a controversy arose regarding the Christian Brothers who, as a result, left the town and in deep frustration at what happened some parishioners wrecked the school and its contents.

It is my wish that the book will give both an interesting and comprehensive picture of Canon Sheehan who as a priest was much loved by the people he served and who as a writer brought great enjoyment to his readers.

Michael Barry

CHAPTER ONE

Patrick Augustine Sheehan was born at No. 29 New Street (now William O'Brien Street) Mallow, Co. Cork on the 17th March 1852. A plaque on the front wall of the house where he was born says that "*Canon Sheehan was born in this house 17 March 1852, died Oct. 5 1913. Dílis do Dhia Dílis d'Éirinn.*" He has invariably been referred to as 'Canon Sheehan of Doneraile'. This arose from the fact that he wrote all his major works while there as Parish Priest. However, Mallow his birthplace, was a town he loved dearly and of which he wrote in later years with great affection pointing out in a letter to his friend and literary critic, Fr. Matthew Russell, S.J. that his home town could lay claim to many famous people.

> *What do you think of this? The Church - Archbishop Purcell; the Law - the late Lord Chancellor Sir Edward Sullivan; Medicine - Sir Richard Quain; Literature and Politics - Thomas Davis and William O'Brien.*

Canon Sheehan's father was also called Patrick and his mother's maiden name was Johana Regan who came from a family widely connected with the Mourne Abbey area. Young Patrick was baptised in St. Mary's Church in Mallow, the sponsors being Mary Anne Relihan and Timothy Cronin. All references up to recently pointed to a family of five children, three boys and two girls. However, in a 1988 indexing of the Mallow Parish Records, it was shown that there were six children in the Sheehan family as follows:

Margaret baptised 16th May 1846; Johana baptised 16th January 1848; Margaret Mary baptised 5th May 1850; Patrick baptised 17th March 1852; Denis baptised 4th June 1854. There was another boy named John who died aged 5½ years. He was not baptised in Mallow. The Mallow Parish Records show a number of different spellings of the name Sheehan. For example, Margaret Mary's surname was spelled Sheahane while Patrick's own surname was given as Sheahan, although he always spelled his name as Sheehan. The family grave in St. Mary's Churchyard, Mallow has a headstone over it with the inscription as follows:

ERECTED BY THE REV P A SHEAHAN AND DENIS B SHEAHAN

IN MEMORY OF THEIR BELOVED PARENTS

PATRICK SHEAHAN WHO DIED JULY 1863

AND HIS WIFE WHO DIED FEBRUARY 6 1864

HERE TOO REPOSE THE REMAINS OF THEIR BROTHER JOHN

WHO DIED AT THE AGE OF FIVE YEARS SIX MONTHS.

MAY THEY REST IN PEACE.

Although there appears to be no definite record to confirm it, the fact that two 'Margarets' appear in the Mallow baptismal records of the Sheehan family leads one to deduce that the Margaret shown as the eldest and born in 1846 most probably died at a very early age leaving Johana (Hannah) born in 1848 then as the eldest of the family. A child born in 1850 was again named Margaret with Mary added to the name. A further strengthening of this deduction is seen later in reference to convent records.

The Sheehan family were in comfortable circumstances. Young Patrick received his early education at the Long Room National School in Mallow where one of his classmates was William O'Brien later to become a noted journalist and parliamentarian. They remained great friends throughout Sheehan's lifetime. Writing about him in his early school days William O'Brien had this to stay:

"Probably he among my school-fellows with whom I should have most in common was the Rev. Dr. Sheehan of later days - poet, mystic, novelist and homilist - most delightful of companions in his books, but in his unformed school-days as pale, diffident and moonstruck as myself."

William O'Brien also refers to that school on the first floor of the Long Room in the Spa Walk in his recollections:

The Long Room, in the days of its pride, was the casino or assembly-room where the Grattans and Ned Lysaghts proferred snuff boxes and sat at the card-tables and danced minuets in the evenings, after drinking the waters and exchanging scandal with the wits and beauties at the Pump-Room in the Spa Glen during the day.

The schoolmaster (O'Connor) was a man of remarkable capacity, an upright ecclesiastically-minded man, who, had he found the right groove, would have made a Bishop of commanding ability and dignity, but having slipped into the wrong one, sank into a disappointed and irascible pedagogue, at war with his parish-priest and regarded by his pupils pretty much as Attilla must have been regarded by his defenceless victims on the plains of Lombardy.

Patrick Sheehan recalled that same teacher Michael Francis O'Connor as a man who emphasised his teaching by 'frequent appeals to the ferrule.' The young school boy received his first musical lessons in the local church choir from one of the curates, Father Patrick Horgan. That priest's nephew was the late John J. Horgan, well known solicitor in Cork and Chairman of the Cork Harbour Commissioners for many years. He too became a very great friend of Canon Sheehan and in an article in the *Irish Monthly*, Mr. Horgan referred to the choir:

My Uncle, who was then curate at Mallow often told me of how he gave Canon Sheehan his first musical lessons in the Church choir. Readers of *My New Curate* will remember the village choir over which Father Letheby presided, and how he 'brought' clear to the front the sweet trebles of the schoolboys on whom he said 'all his hopes depended'.

The young Sheehan's youthful days in Mallow are recalled with nostalgia in his own fine essay *Moonlight of Memory*.

How beautifully, for example do the plain, prosaic, limestone walls of the old Market House in Mallow, which crowned and terminated the New Street in which I was born stand out...... How well I remember it in the sunlight and in the moonlight...... the vast and tremendous circuses whose splendours, as of Arabian Nights, were hidden within under locked and closed gates.

When Patrick Sheehan was growing up in Mallow, the Fenian movement was beginning to take shape with men secretly drilling and marching in the woods round about. That period of history remained ingrained in the young boy's mind culminating in a book he completed some time before he died called *The Graves At Kilmorna* and which wasn't published until about eighteen months after his death. In the essay already referred to, he described the Fenians of his youth as:

> silent strong men into whose character some stern and terrible energy seemed to have been infused. There were no braggarts among them. Their passion was too deep for words; and that passion was an all-consuming, fierce unswerving love for Ireland.

The town of Sheehan's boyhood leaps to life in the pen picture he paints. Although as a boy he was no great sporting participant, sport held a keen interest for him. He tells us that when growing up in Mallow, football was almost unknown. Hurling and handball were played in the Winter and in Summer it was cricket.

> Every lane, every street had its cricket club; and high above all and dominating all was the M.C.C., the magic letters that floated on the flag that hung above the little shanty in the cricket field that lies to the east of the monastery. That Club was the most formidable in the South of Ireland.

Nostalgically he recalled his cricket heroes:

> Curtin, the Captain. George and Henry Foott demon bowlers; Pat Kelly, the slow bowler whose deadly 'twists' were feared more than the canonading of the Footts; Jos Mullane, the famous backstop. Micka Roche, the favourite batsman and Bill O'Brien, the genial giant whose mighty feat of sending a ball over the Courthouse walls from the centre of the cricket grounds is remembered to this day.

The essay *Moonlight of Memory* is to a great extent the biography of the youthful years of Patrick Sheehan. It is an account of his life and times in Mallow during a turbulent period in Irish history. His great love for the town of his birth and of the people who lived there enhances the very descriptive passages of the essay. He tells us also that as a boy in Mallow the relations between Protestant and Catholic

10

were 'exceedingly happy and cordial'. It is, however, the 'characters' in the Mallow of his youth that he liked to recall most of all.

> During the Summer evenings, a little man, clad like a sailor in blue blouse and white nankeen or lined trousers used to put in an appearance just at the corner of Fair Street and right opposite the entrance gate to the Protestant Church. His face was deeply marked and he looked insignificant enough; but his feats of strength, for it was these he came to exhibit, hoping to earn a few pence thereby, were very remarkable and showed uncommon muscular and nervous power. ......the humble, yet picturesque celebrities who haunted the streets of Mallow during these days and who came prominently to the front during election times and were well known at fair, market and cross:- Bill Shehane, the giant who always inherited the boots and cast-off integuments of another giant, old Homan Haines; Bill Shehane who knocked down with one blow a famous and dangerous bull in the Big Meadow and then cried chivalrously "Get up you, you son of a gun. I never struck a man down"; Stephen the Fool, who once swallowed a live mouse for the premium of six pence and the delectation of the Club gentlemen; Jack the Manager; Davy the Lady; Biddy Black, Peg Mack, Ellen Gorman of the Cakes; and last-not-least, Kitty Moss, the terror of our childhood.

They were the characters who put an indelible mark on the boyhood days of Patrick Sheehan, a boyhood that was enhanced too by some of the clergy such as Fathers Justin McCarthy, Abbe Moriarty, Danger Murphy, Denis O'Connell and Patrick Horgan.

The carefree days of young Sheehan took a severe jolt when in the Summer of 1863 his father died and in February of the following year his mother passed away. At the time of their deaths, the parish priest of Mallow was Rev. John McCarthy, a brother of the previous P.P. and who now became guardian of the four children with 'an income from a modest property'. The security of the home was shattered but Patrick's two sisters Johanna and Margaret did everything possible to alleviate the distress. They were eventually sent to the Loreto Convent in Fermoy to further their education.

Patrick was aged fourteen when he came to St. Colman's College in Fermoy. The date was the 6th April 1866. As well as being a Secondary School, St. Colman's was the Diocesan Seminary for Cloyne and had only opened its doors for the first time about eight years previously. The Mallow youth had thoughts of the priesthood from early on although it was said that he showed an interest at one stage in law but was advised against it.

Patrick Sheehan was a very bright student in St. Colman's College, one of the top pupils of his time. His entry to the College coincided with the preparation of the Fenian Rebellion of 1867.

It amused us, young rebels in St. Colman's, to see or pretend we saw the dark files of the Fenians silhoutted against the virgin-ground of the hills and the red patches of the British Regiments in the rear.

The grim reality of that period was highlighted for him in the Spring of 1867 following the death in Kilclooney Wood of the well known Fenian Peter O'Neill-Crowley. The funeral cortege passed through Fermoy and in *Moonlight of Memory* young Sheehan recalled that scene:

"I remember well that evening on which that remarkable funeral took place. It was computed that at least five thousand men took part in the procession; and shouldered the coffin of the dead patriot over mountain and valley and river until they placed the sacred burden down there near the sea and under the shadow of the church at Ballymacoda. I remember how a group of us young lads, shivered in the cold March wind there on the College Terrace at Fermoy and watched the dark masses of men swaying over the Bridge, the yellow coffin conspicuous in their midst. We caught another glimpse of the funeral cortege as it passed Sergeant's lodge; then we turned away with tears of sorrow and anger in our eyes.

The year 1868 was a good academic year for the young student. In the Summer term he headed the honours class in History, Greek, English Composition, Geometry and Algebra. To those he added a second in

12

Christian Doctrine and a third in Latin. All in all it was a creditable performance.

However, academic success was to be overshadowed by further tragedy in 1869. His sister Margaret had entered The Convent of Mercy, Mallow in 1867, a year after her sister Hannah had entered there. The cursed disease of consumption was then rampant. Margaret Sheehan was professed by special dispensation on her death-bed on 1st October 1869 to become Sister Mary Augustine. Sadly, she died on that day also.

The Register record of the Convent of Mercy, Mallow tells us that Hannah Sheehan received the 'Holy Habit' on the 8th December 1866 and was professed on the 8th December 1868, the year that her sister Margaret received the 'Holy Habit'.

An interesting extract from the Mallow Convent Annals is as follows:

> "In 1866, a number of Postulants entered the growing Community. The Misses O'Toole, Holden, Sheehan, Conway and Keane, who later with the Reception of the Habit became:
> Sr. Mary Theresa O'Toole, afterwards Mother M. Francis - a native of Birr.
> Sr. M. Holden - of New Ross
> Sr. M. Stanislaus - of Mallow
> Sr. M. Genevieve - of Meelin Parish
> Sr. M. Camilus - of Birr
>
> During the following year, Margaret Sheehan (a sister of Sr. M. Stanislaus above & of the later famous Priest-Novelist - Canon P.A. Sheehan) joined the Community.
> This younger nun received St. Augustine as her Patron. Neither sister was to live long, for Sr. M. Augustine was professed on her death-bed in October 1869 & Sister M. Stanislaus died on 17 December 1871, long before their illustrious brother returned as curate to his native Mallow".

The fact that this extract refers to Margaret Sheehan as 'This younger nun' strengthens the deducation that the Margaret Sheehan (first born) must have died in infancy.

The death of his younger sister coming so soon after that of his parents was a severe blow to young Patrick. He himself was never of robust constitution and all through his life poor health dogged him. When he completed his studies at St. Colman's College, the Seminary in Maynooth was his next step. He had hoped to get a place at the Irish College in Rome but this did not materialise. Instead at the end of August 1869, he entered St. Patrick's College, Maynooth to study for the priesthood having received one of two vacancies for the diocese of Cloyne that year.

His academic relationship with St. Colman's had ended but he maintained contact with it throughout his life. He had been extremely happy there and had great affection for his old Alma Mater. He was responsible, through the contributions he gave from his literary income, especially in his early years of authorship, for building the College chapel. Acknowledgement of this is recorded on the memorial tablet at the chapel entrance which reads as follows:

In grateful memory of

VERY REV. P. A. CANON SHEEHAN, D.D., P.P.

Doneraile

whose generosity largely helped to build

this chapel

He died October 5, 1913.

By order of

THE MOST REV. R. BROWNE D.D.

Lord Bishop of Cloyne

An Anniversary Requiem Mass

is to be celebrated for the repose

of his soul on the 5th day of October

each year.

R. I. P.

The records of Maynooth throw little light on Sheehan the student who one day would become an international literary figure. He may have been overshadowed by the academic greats of that era in the seminary and it wasn't until he was ordained that he was able to come to the surface and carve his own niche in the Ireland of his time.

A colleague of Sheehan's in Maynooth writing later of the great students of his day mentioned that "you had men like Canon Sheehan, who scarcely uttered a word, but read the heavens."

Many years later, Sheehan's great friend and literary adviser Fr. Matthew Russell, S. J. had this to say:

> It remains a puzzle to most men who knew Canon Sheehan in after days and realised that his literary work as well as his pastoral wisdom were in truth the fruit of a laborious and close application of the years spent in the Seminary, how a youth of such exceptional ability was able to escape distinction during his Maynooth courses so completely that, since he has become famous, many who were almost his contemporaries at college have been slow to believe that he ever was a student at Maynooth.

Patrick Sheehan was a brilliant young man, probably one of the brightest of his generation in Maynooth but his reticence, his unassuming way and also of course his indifferent health, all militated against him attracting special attention.

When he entered Maynooth in 1869, it was at a time of great change for that institution. Opened under an Act of the old Irish Parliament in 1795, Maynooth had been in receipt of an annual grant from the Crown under Pitt's Ministry. The grant was £8,928 a year. Following the Act of Union, the grant was continued. Sir Robert Peel got a Bill through the British Parliament giving Maynooth a permanent endowment of £26,000 a year and added to this was a grant of £30,000 for building purposes.

In 1869, with the passing of the Irish Church Act under Gladstone, the permanent endowment was withdrawn and a temporary subsidy was granted. The passing of the Act also put control of the College under the authority of the Roman Catholic Bishops. This posed many initial financial problems and the granting of free studentships and exhibitions had to cease. Changes in the constitution and rules governing the College became necessary and also to the syllabus taught and to the teaching staff.

Sheehan commenced his studies under all this upheavel. His years at Maynooth cannot be classed as the happiest and his opinions of its educational system were not, as we shall see later, always complimentary. He was an avid reader and as a student he had limited access to the great works of literature in the college library. It was there that his enquiring and receptive mind began to extend its boundaries, thus laying the foundation for later study of many of the great writers. Referring to this many years later he wrote:

> Far back in the 'sixties, literature had to be read surreptitiously ... It was a serious thing to be detected in such clandestine studies and I dare say our superiors were quite right in insisting that we should rigidly adhere to the system of pure Scholasticism which was a college tradition.

Nevertheless, he found 'his scholastic studies dry and uninteresting, not understanding their application and practical importance.'

He was a very diligent student in Maynooth but the intense study and reading which he engaged in soon began to tell on his health and he was forced to spend periods in the college infirmary. Again tragedy struck the young clerical student with the serious illness of his sister Hannah then Sister Stanislaus in the Sisters of Mercy Convent in Mallow. Being the eldest of the family, it was to her mainly that he was able to turn to following the death of his parents. At the time of her illness she was Directress of the National Schools attached to the Convent and was both a talented teacher and administrator.

It was in the year 1871 that Hannah Sheehan became seriously stricken with consumption, the disease which had claimed her sister a few years before. She had kept the seriousness of her illness from Patrick to avoid worrying him. Sadly, when her end drew near in December of that year, he himself was ill in the Maynooth infirmary and was unable to be at her bedside when she passed away on the 17th December 1871. It was a devastating blow to him. He had been deeply attached to both his sisters and kept woven strands of their hair in a small leather frame during his lifetime.

That he could not be with Hannah at the time of her death had a deep affect on him. Many years later when he was writing his second novel, *The Triumph Of Failure*, the memory of the tragic death of his sister came back very clearly to him. A friend happened to visit him as he was working on his book and found him in tears. He queried him on his grief only to be told that at that particular time of writing, he was putting on paper the death scene of a very lovable character called Alice Dean. It had recalled vividly for him, he said, the death of his sister Hannah.

Sheehan's essay *Moonlight of Memory* which tells us so much about his youth does not give us any inkling of his home life or of his relationship with his parents but we do learn something from his fine work *Under The Cedars And The Stars* where he says:

> Strange I never feel the proximity of father or mother but my sisters - one in particular, the only dark-haired in the family, has haunted me through life. I no more doubt of her presence and her light touch on the issues of my life than I doubt of the breath of wind that flutters the tassel of my biretta in my hand. Yet what is strange is not her nearness but her farness. I should not be in the least surprised if I saw her face shining swiftly from the darkness, or saw her form outlined against the twilight sky. But only I cannot speak to her, or touch her, there is the problem and the vexation.

Following the death of his sister Hannah, "the only dark-haired in the family" recurring ill health forced him to leave Maynooth for the entire 1872-1873 period and he returned home to Mallow. This was an additional source of worry to him and cast doubts on his ability to handle the onerous tasks of the priesthood. He returned again to Maynooth for the 1873-1874 term and completed his studies taking First in Sacred Scripture and in Dogmatic Theology together with Sixth in Moral Theology. It was a considerable achievement for a student with such a sick record. Although his course in Maynooth was now complete, he was too young to be ordained and he returned to Mallow where his guardian Fr. John McCarthy was still Parish Priest. It was a good opportunity for the student priest to study at first hand the workings of a parish and he assisted the clergy in their various duties gaining much valued experience as he went along.

In October of that year 1874, his guardian became Bishop of Cloyne, replacing Dr. Willliam Keane who had run the diocese for the previous seventeen years or so. In April 1875, Patrick Sheehan was asked to attend a retreat in preparation for his ordination at the Vincentian Monastery, Sundays Well Cork.

He was ordained in St. Mary's Cathedral Cork on Sunday 18th April 1875 by Bishop Delaney. It is not clear as to where the young priest celebrated his first Mass but it is thought that it was in the Convent of Mercy Mallow. There was no vacancy as yet for him in the Cloyne Diocese and he was assigned to the English Mission.

CHAPTER TWO

Father Sheehan began his priestly ministry on the Cathedral staff at Plymouth which was then under the guidance of Bishop William Vaughan. Canon Herbert Wollett was the Rector of the Cathedral and the young Irish priest was full of hope and zeal, coupled with the diffidence of a raw missionary from the seminary in Maynooth. He was now in another land, the majority of its population not of his religious persuasion. Plymouth was a noisy port town where in its seamier quarters drunken sailors and prostitutes consorted.

He worked extremely hard, conscientiously gaining worthwhile experience. Close to where the river Tamar entered the sea was the naval hospital at Stonehouse where he was obliged to go and attend to the sick and dying. His novel *Luke Delmege* reflected many of his own experiences of those days.

He had been in Plymouth only three months when he was transferred to Exeter. The rector there was Canon Hobson who apparently at that particular time in his priestly life thought he had a vocation for a religious order and went away for about a year, leaving Fr. Sheehan to run the parish. One of his duties was to celebrate Mass in Dartmoor prison in the absence of the prison chaplain.

The grim edifice had been built in 1806 during the Napoleonic War and was used to house war prisoners. Although it was abandoned at the end of that period, the building was converted to a convict prison in 1855. At the time of Fr. Sheehan's ministry in Exeter, Michael Davitt was a prisoner in Dartmoor. Davitt's parents had been evicted from their home in Co. Mayo in 1853 and the entire family moved to Haslingden in Lancashire where the young Michael went to work in a mill at an early age. It was there that he lost an arm when it got caught in machinery. He joined the Fenians and was arrested in 1870 on the evidence of an informer. He was sentenced to fifteen years penal servitude but was freed in 1878. There is no record that the prisoner and Fr. Sheehan ever met, although he was recognised by the latter, because of his missing arm, while the priest was preparing to say Mass.

Those visits to Dartmoor had a profound affect on Fr. Sheehan and in his book *The Graves at Kilmorna*, his description of Dartmoor and its fettered convicts leap from the pages with startling clarity.

His duties at Exeter were very onerous and for health reasons he was obliged to take a short holiday in the Summer of 1876 and went on a visit to Lourdes.

Father Sheehan appeared to have mixed feelings with regard to his experiences there. Much to his surprise, he found a deep faith but there were many things he didn't like.

"He met the old disappointments where he had looked for consistency. Thus at the bookstalls in Lourdes, he discovered that, alongside the devotional books which the pilgrims were expected to purchase, by far the largest number of works on sale were those of Dumas and George Sands."

He returned to Exeter feeling much better in health and undertook his parish work with vigour. He was gaining considerable experience through his attachment to organisations such as St. Vincent de Paul and saw at first hand the levels to which people sank not alone through poverty but also through gambling, drink, prostitution and so on. Many from his own country were among them. He saw a sharp contrast between the English and their Irish counterparts where thrift and cleanliness were concerned and he tried his best to redress these failings.

Father Sheehan was in many ways an academic and was as much at home, if not more so, among men of letters as he was among ordinary people. In Exeter, while standing in for the highly educated and respected Canon Hobson, the Irish Priest was invited to many cultured functions. The Canon belonged to a very august body of men drawn from the fields of literature, the arts and science who met regularly in a refined atmosphere to discuss and debate their interests. Father Sheehan's invitation to join them enabled him to get a far greater understanding of the English character than heretofore.

He had fixed ideas coming from Ireland not alone regarding the English in general but on English clergy too. Because of the contacts he was now making, he began to see them in a different light. He began to make comparisons between both peoples, lay and cleric and the results were'nt always favourable to his own. Such comparisons were to create a barrier for a while between himself and his parishioners when he first returned home to the Cloyne diocese.

There was of course the extremely formal manner of the English which took some time to come to terms with and there was their punctuality. If Mass was at eight a.m. then it started precisely at that hour. It took him some time to adjust to all this but when he did, he saw the merit in much of what the likeable Canon Hobson had been doing. He even saw himself trying to promote some changes back home when he got his first curacy there. He had learned much and would be returning to his own diocese, hopefully with a more open and developed mind. He had been well appreciated in Exeter as a priest and also as a man who was more than anxious to work for the betterment of the community in general. This was borne out close on forty years later when, after his death, in response to queries by his first biographer Fr. Heuser, to Fr. W. J. Hegarty who was then serving at Holy Cross Church, Plymouth, some interesting observations were made about Fr. Sheehan and the impressions he had made on the people he had served during his period on the English Mission.

> ... he was appointed curate to the late Provost of Exeter, Mgr. Hobson ... I was sent as curate to Exeter in 1912 and there was still a little group of old people who remembered "Fr. Sheehan" quite well. He seems to have made pretty well the same impression on all. The general verdict was that he was a man of more than ordinary piety, that he was intensly observant and no detail was too small to escape his notice. He was generally recognised to have been even in these early days a splendid preacher, his chief characteristics being consciceness and brevity. ... In particular they told me of his first sermon. He preached on charity, the sermon lasted three minutes and yet close on forty years afterwards, I heard the general outline reproduced by a woman of 88, who had heard him deliver.

Referring to Fr. Sheehan's own recollections of the people of Exeter, Fr. Hegarty wrote:

A few months before his death (I was then curate of Exeter) he wrote to me in reply to a letter which I had sent him. The accuracy of his recollections astonished me. He could almost give you the dimensions of the houses where he used to visit. The little peculiarities and eccentricities of individuals who in his day had been boys and girls and in mine had developed into dignified fathers and stately matrons he could bring out with marvellous accuracy and humour. His own verdict of his time there was that he was under an everlasting debt to England. In a letter to me he wrote thus:

"During my curacy at Exeter I learned more theology than I had learned during my whole college career and gained more experience than I have gained during the long years that have since elapsed."

CHAPTER THREE

Father Sheehan's time on the English Mission came to a close in 1877 when the Bishop of Cloyne, Dr. McCarthy recalled him to take up duty as Junior curate in his home town of Mallow. He replaced Fr. John Lynch and lived for a while at Bath View, close to the Convent School. The parish priest was Archdeacon Regan who was also Vicar General of the diocese. There were two other curates in the parish, Father Alex Morrisey and Father Edmund Morton. Settling in to a new parish, the first in his own country wasn't easy, even if that parish was his native one. He had spent sufficient time with English colleagues to have absorbed aspects of their culture that would be found to be somewhat alien among his own people. However, much of what he had seen and heard he saw as beneficial and of considerable advantage should he be able to put it into practice at home. Later, his writings would suggest that were he to have been left in England, he would not have been unhappy. In *Luke Delmege* we are reminded of this in a conversation between the two priest characters - Father Luke Delmege and Father Sheldon.

> "I've made up my mind" said Luke continuing "that my work
> lies here in England. Everything points to it. So far, I have
> been fairly successful; and I have no doubt but that a wider
> and more - well useful career lies before me. .... "You see,
> everything in Ireland is fixed in a cast iron mould. They don't
> understand change which is in progress.
> Everything is judged by age. ... No one asks: "What can you
> do? or what have you done?" But "How old are you? How
> long have you been on the Mission?" - result: After a few
> spasmodic efforts, you become convulsive, you sink into a
> lethargy, from which there is no awakening. You become
> aged, not by years but by despair."

Father Sheehan accepted his call to return home with mixed feelings. He was now only a Junior curate and of course hadn't the authority he experienced in England. Nevertheless, he set out to do his best and implement if possible what he had come to admire in the English Catholic Church. It wasn't to be easy. With only a couple of years priestly experience behind him and that in another country, he was inclined to move too fast making changes here and there.

Slowly he came to grips with his work as a curate in Mallow. Apart from his spiritual duties and responsibilities, one of his main interests was the youth. These he saw as Ireland's only hope for the future and if their energies could be properly harnessed, then there was hope. He felt that a sound basic education was of prime importance. At this very early period of his priestly life, we see his great love of books and literature percolating through, a love that he strove to pass on to those with whom he came into contact.

With reference to education, Father Sheehan did not make a very auspicious beginning in his native Mallow. In fact, he walked into a sea of trouble. Away back in 1864, the Rev. John McCarthy, then Parish Priest of Mallow and later to become Bishop of Cloyne had invited the Christian Brothers to set up a primary school in the town which they did in 1868. Things went smoothly for ten years or so and then in 1878 a degree of animosity appeared to grow towards the Christian Brothers by a few priests in the diocese. In Mallow it developed into a very bitter dispute between the then Parish Priest Archdeacon Regan and some of the clergy on the one hand and the parishioners on the other.

It transpired that early in 1878 Brother Jerome Murphy was being transferred from Fermoy to Mallow and a committee was formed to present a testimonial to the departing Brother. One of the recepients of a circular regarding the testimonial was Fr. O'Callaghan, a local curate in Fermoy. The tone of his reply to the secretary of the committee indicates the degree of undercurrent existing at the time.

The Presbytery,
18th Jan. 1878.

Mr. Kelleher,
Patrick St. , Fermoy.

I have to acknowledge receipt of your circular in the matter of the proposed testimonial to Brother Murphy and beg to inform you in reply thereto, that I would much prefer you had seen fit not to trouble me with your favour, as I can be no party in paying publicly, what I believe to be, an undeserved compliment.

I must decline participation in the whitewashing process to which Mr. Murphy would have himself subjected on his way to his new home. ... Besides, I find it laid down in the Papal Constitution on which the Christian Brothers Institute depends for existence that the Brothers are prohibited from receiving any reward or gift from pupils or parents and I am not aware of any special privilege being granted to Mr. Murphy.

With the action of others in the affair, I have no concern: as long as they only speak for themselves and of themselves they are perfectly within their rights; but if anyone should have the bad taste to do otherwise, I am quite certain there are many of my way of thinking who will not permit themselves to be involved, even indirectly and thereby give the movement a fictitious importance.

I am, Sir,
Yours, etc.

P. J. O'Callaghan, C.C.

It was the beginning of what became an extremely serious issue in the parish of Mallow between priests and people. While undoubtedly there were personality clashes, there were also fundamental issues involved. The principal one was that the Christian Brothers did not come under the control of the Bishop and priests of a diocese in which they had schools. Maynooth had tried to change this situation

25

regarding the Brothers in 1875 with the passing of Maynooth Decrees. The Christian Brothers regarded these Decrees as a violation of the rights and privileges conferred on them by their brief of Approbation and they accordingly appealed to Rome. The decision came back in their favour. The Irish Bishops were not satisfied and had the case re-opened. The second decision was, as before, in favour of the Christian Brothers. It was while the second appeal was pending that the trouble arose in Mallow. The end result was that the Brothers felt they were not wanted by the clergy there and accordingly left the town. The parishioners were outraged at this and a group of them took over the school. Later, as the dispute intensified, the group wrecked the school and destroyed its contents. It was a black chapter in the history of Mallow parish.

As already mentioned, Father Sheehan was a junior curate there at that time and was caught up in the upheaval. During the period when the school was in the possession of the parishioners, the Bishop, Dr. Mccarthy directed his priests "to call on those who amongst the people respect authority, to separate themselves from those who have taken part in those scandalous proceedings and thus escape the punishment which I feel it my duty to inflict on them. Meantime, I hereby make it a reserved sin, which no Confessor can absolve from, to hold possession of those schools and this reservation extends to all those who have counselled or directed them in those proceedings."

Expressing the Bishop's directive on the following Sunday Father Sheehan came out strongly and said from the altar:

"It is all very well to say that Monks and Christian Brothers were holy men but he could tell them, if they read ecclesiastical history, they would see that the great heresies which had scourged the Church had been nurtured in the hearts and sprung from the lips and writings of monks."

His remarks were quoted in the press and actually attributed to one of the other Mallow curates, Father Morrisey who in fact replied by letter to the paper in question pointing out that he had not said Mass in Mallow on the Sunday referred to and so could not have preached the sermon quoted in the paper.

The remarks made by Father Sheehan resulted from the impetuosity of a young curate and were very much regretted by him later when he became a true friend and admirer of the Christian Brothers in Doneraile, having seen the great work they were doing in the field of education. The following verses were later penned to commemorate the Mallow Christian Brothers' school episode:

MALLOW CHRISTIAN BROTHERS SCHOOL

I fought at Balaclava, I fought at Inkerman
I stood the brazen Malekoff, I stood at the Redan
I'd rather fight them o'er again and front Sebastapool
Then face the bold defenders of the Christian Brothers School.

Their shouts were "No Surrender, the Cross shall ne'er come down"
Whoever dare offend it will face a peoples' frown
For we're the Rakes of Mallow whose blood will never cool
While insult dares to threaten the Christian Brothers School.

A posse of policemen came trotting to the ground
With a gallant staff of 'North Cork', with many a cartridge round
Though well they were provided with mass destruction's tools
We asked them for no quarter at the Christian Brothers School.

The balls of malediction from other quarters flew
But bravely we defied them and did their authors too
'Twas said we were "no Catholics but base rebellious fools"
And we'd not yield to Government our Christian Brothers School.

I hope to se through Ireland if wanting it should be
Such men to back the people as did our Committee
'Tis Irish Education can win for us Home Rule
If we rise to be a nation, let us thank the Brothers School.

I'm proud of you my native town, your schoolboys and your men
And hope to see in Mallow soon the Brothers back again
We'll then repair their dwelling house, their shattered desks and stool
And we'll expel the foreigners from our Christian Brothers School.

The Patrician brothers replaced the Christian Brothers in Mallow and slowly things normalised in the parish. In 1880 Father Sheehan formed a Literary Society in the town, specifically aimed at the Catholic youth. It was a society which as he himself said was founded

> not with "the intention of making this Institute a mere place of amusement where a few hours may be spent with pleasure, but without profit. We have a higher ambition. We desire to make it the means of supplying to you a knowledge of all those subjects that are interesting to the modern world and are familiar to the minds of educated men."

The words were part of his inaugural address to the Mallow Literary Society which was entitled *Irish Youth And High Ideals* given on the 11th November, 1880. The lecture was a long and rather deep thinking philosophical talk, much of which was more suited to University students than to the youth of a country town. He did however hammer home the benefits that education could bring and that a sound appreciation of literature would enable one pick out not alone what was good but also what was false.

Around this time changes were coming about in Irish education. Jobs in areas such as the Civil Service were being opened up to competition by the Government. Father Sheehan's younger brother, Denis Bernard, obtained a post in Local Government through open competition. The former however wasn't happy with some of the recent developments in education. He was critical of the passing of the Intermediate Education Act of 1878 and saw in it a move towards the secularisation of the education of the Irish people. Father Sheehan wrote at the time:

> The Tories have outwitted the Irish priesthood at last. They have introduced into the Primary and Secondary Schools - and they will introduce into the University Scheme, the system of payment by results. The consequence will be that in a short time your whole educational system in Ireland, from the lowest bench in the country school to the *aula maxima* of the University, will be thoroughly secularised.

The Literary Society in Mallow had been well established when early in the year 1881, he was called by the Bishop to take up duty in Cobh, then called Queenstown.

CHAPTER FOUR

Father Sheehan took up duty in Cobh early in March 1881, a town where his former guardian Bishop McCarthy now resided. It was a big change from the inland and rural town of Mallow. Cobh was then a British naval base, akin to his first posting to Plymouth. The former, however, was more than just a naval base, it was also the gateway to the western world. Ever since the mass emigration following the famine, Cobh had witnessed the countless partings from loved ones as men, women and children set out for the new world in search of a better life. Most of them would never return and it was on the windswept quayside of that southern Irish port that Father Sheehan was to witness for the next seven years or so the heart-rending plight of so many of his countrymen. Here the stark reality of emigration faced him and highlighted the necessity of a thorough grinding in the faith of those who were leaving Ireland for the materialistic land of opportunity, America. He wasn't at all happy with what he was witnessing. His country's hopes and aspirations for the future were taking a severe knock as young boys and girls left their native land and then sending for other members of their families once they themselves had become established and secure.

Pastoral work always took pride of place with Father Sheehan and he threw himself wholeheartedly into the task before him. Nevertheless, he also saw the power of the pen through the wide vista of his reading and he began to use it . He had from time to time contributed articles to local publications but not to the quality journals of the day. It was in Cobh that he began this exercise and found it to be a long hard road. He was hopeful that his writing would attract the attention of his clerical colleagues, this wasn't so and he was disappointed.

The pace at which he was driving himself began to affect his health. His concern for the poor and the needy was very great and he was often to be seen in the poorer quarters of the town trying to alleviate the harsh conditions under which many were then living. Because of its location as a trans-atlantic port, its population increased enormously at times due to the gathering of emigrants there. This only served to increase the existing hardships and put greater strain on the limited resources of the many organisations engaged in social services.

A cursary glance at Father Sheehan in those days, in fact, at any time of his priestly life, would lead one to assume that he would be more at home in the great halls of learning than in the slums. Yet it would be a very wrong assumption. In fact he was an extremely humble man and also a very charitable one who, when he died, all the older generations had instances of his unostentatious kindness, especially to the poor and the sick. Despite his busy pastoral life he was often asked to speak in Churches in Cork and Limerick and he invariably obliged. In fact later on as his fame as a writer grew, the invitations to lecture also grew. Eventually pressure of work in Cobh took its toll and he had to be relieved of all pastoral duties for the year 1888.

To recuperate, he spent a considerable time in Glengariff later moving to Youghal. While away from the bustle of Cobh he had ample time to devote to thinking and writing. Much of his time was spent in commune with nature and an old friend of his Canon Keller of Youghal recalling him many years later said that in those days Father Sheehan would be absent for hours and when he would go and look for him "he would find him standing like one in a trance looking out upon the wild waste of the winter sea."

Canon Daniel Keller, later to become a Dean of the Diocese of Cloyne had come as Parish Priest to Cobh in 1881, moving to Youghal in 1885 where he served until his death in November 1922. The two men had become close friends while in Cobh. At the time of Father Sheehan's convalescence the country was in turmoil due to land agitation. It was the Land League period. Many clergy throughout the country were deeply involved as leaders of the tenant farmers in their respective areas. They attended meetings, made speeches and displayed their sympathies with the Land League and later on with the Plan of Campaign which had been waged since 1886. It was in 1888 too that a Papal Prescript was issued which condemned the Plan of Campaign and boycott which had been so effective against unscrupulous landlords. This brought much antagonism between the people and many Catholic Church leaders.

Canon Keller, was very involved in the Land War. Because of his close friendship with the Youghal P.P. Father Sheehan would have learned much regarding the land problems from him and this material would prove to be of considerable use for his books in the years ahead. In March 1887, as leader of landlord Ponsonby's tenants, Canon Keller had refused to attend a court hearing in Dublin and identify the trustees of the tenant's 'war chest' accumulated during the operation of the Plan of Campaign. Because of his refusal, he was arrested and imprisoned in Kilmainham.

Father Sheehan himself had no direct involvement with the Land League. Due to his indifferent health, he certainly wouldn't have had the capacity to handle the intense agitation between tenants and landlords. Also of course, he would in many ways rank among the conservative churchmen of his day in his approach towards the breaking of laws, however repugnant such laws may have been. As will be seen later, he became actively involved in assisting many of his Doneraile parishioners in their negotiations with the landlords following the passing of the Land Acts.

He made a good recovery but nevertheless the Bishop, Dr. McCarthy, thought it best for his health that he should leave Cobh and return to his native Mallow this time as senior curate. It was in the year 1890 that he took up duty there again. There were two other curates in the town, Father William Coughlan and Father David Barry. Archdeacon Regan was still Parish Priest but was replaced the following year by Canon John S. Wigmore, V.F.

Father Sheehan was now thirty six and much more mature than he had been during his first assignment in the town. He continued where he had left off some years before in the organisation of many activities. Many children of his earlier curacy in Mallow were now young men and women, some had even taken the emigrant ship. Much of what he had set up in the literary field had fallen through and this he revived.

His return marked the beginning of a new phase in his literary work. While his literary life will be discussed in detail at a later stage, it is appropriate here to point out that what had been up to then a very intellectual approach to literature in his essays and literary criticisms etc., he now began in earnest to consider the use of his pen as a possible means of spreading the Christian message through short stories, poems, articles and ultimately novels. Through these media he hoped not alone to entertain but to highlight what was both good and bad in Irish society and endeavour to sow the seeds of change where necessary. A lack of confidence in his ability as a writer in those early years forced him to shun publicity and he was extremely wary of putting his name to material that he had written.

He was sufficiently experienced to know and had a keen intelligent mind to see that the once enormous control the clergy had over the laity was diminishing and he was worried about it. Hence his pen was to aid his stance in the pulpit. In December 1893, his former guardian and Bishop of Cloyne, Dr. McCarthy, died and the new Bishop appointed was Dr. Robert Browne who had been President of Maynooth College. He was consecrated in August 1894. He too was a past pupil of St. Colman's College, Fermoy. Father Sheehan had just left Maynooth when Dr. Brown became Dean there.

In May 1895 Father Sheehan completed the MS of his first novel *Geoffrey Austin, Student.* In that year too he was promoted to Parish Priest of Doneraile. He was a long way from being next in line for promotion, being aged only forty three at the time of his new post.

CHAPTER FIVE

Father Patrick Sheehan took up the post of Parish Priest of Doneraile around the middle of July 1895. He was the second Patrick Sheehan to become P.P. there, the first being parish priest between 1839 and 1849. In a letter to his Jesuit friend in Dublin Fr. Russell, he said:

> ... I am informed that the Bishop intends to advance me this week to the pastoral charge of Doneraile - a pretty town - six miles north of Mallow - just now vacated by the resignation of Fr. Ashlin. It will be a great compliment as there are about 26 priests senior to me in the Diocese.

He was coming to a parish with an ancient Christian heritage where the earliest written account of churches in the Doneraile area was in pre-Norman times in a tract called *Criocadh an Caoille* which described an area corresponding to the present barony of Fermoy. There, written in old Irish, were a number of churches near Doneraile listed - Killada, Clenor, Cahirduggan and Kilcolman.

The Taxation of Pope Nicholas IV in the year 1291 which was a taxation of the goods of the Bishop of Cloyne throughout his diocese was granted by the Pope to King Edward 1 of England for 6 years to help defray the expenses of the Crusade to the Holy Land. The churches near Doneraile referred to in that Taxation were Cahirduggan. Russath (Rossagh), Dunrayle (Doneraile), Clusdugfog (Kilconners, Clenwyr (Clenor) and Sonnachgown (Shanballymore).

Moving along in time to the Penal Laws against Catholics in Ireland (1691 - 1761) the Catholic Church suffered very badly as priests and bishops were banished under an Act which decreed that all Popish Archbishops, Bishops, Vicars General, Deans, Jesuits, Monks, Friars and other regular popish clergy and all papists exercising ecclesiastical jurisdiction, should depart from the Kingdom before the 1st May 1698. A Registration Act was also passed in the reign of Queen Anne dealing with diocesan clergy and this compelled every popish priest then in the country to register in the Court of Sessions held immediately after 24th June 1704.

The first parish priest of Doneraile registered under this Act was Tadgh O Dalaigh, a Gaelic poet who lived at Carker where it was said there was a bardic school. He served in Doneraile from 1686 to 1717. In those days Doneraile parish was referred to as having "a kind of shed for a mass-house". Again the Gaelic tradition was continued in the person of An tAthair Eoghan O Caoimh who was parish priest from 1717 to 1726. He is buried in Oldcourt graveyard in front of the old church at Rossdoyle. His three immediate successors are also buried there:- Fr. John Cotter P.P. (1739-1784): Fr. James Cotter P.P. (1784-1799) and Fr. Lewis Walsh P.P. (1799-1815).

In the late 18th century Doneraile had a chapel located at the end of what is still called Chapel Lane. It had a thatched roof. Following the death of Fr. Walsh in 1815, Dr. William O'Brien took over the parish and within ten years began the building of the present church. The foundation stone was laid on 15th June 1826. The church was built on a site given free by Lord Doneraile who also contributed £146 towards its construction. It was completed in 1827 and dedicated to the Nativity of the Blessed Virgin Mary.

As can be gleaned from his letter to Father Russell, Father Sheehan was extremely pleased with his appointment to Doneraile. He was replacing Rev. Stephen Coppinger Ashlin who had been parish priest in Doneraile for the previous fourteen years. Ill health had forced his retirement. Ironically, he outlived his replacement. In fact, Father Ashlin's retirement lasted twenty three years. He died on the 18th November 1918 at the Alexian Brothers Home, Twyford Abbey, Park Royal, London, where he was buried.

Father Sheehan's feelings on his new appointment can probably be best appreciated from his most famous book MY NEW CURATE:

> ... It happened in this wise. The Bishop, the old man, sent for
> me and said with what I would call a tone of pity or contempt
> - but he was incapable of either, for he was the essence of
> charity and sincerity - "Fr. Dan, you are a bit of a litterateur,
> I understand; Kilronan is vacant. You'll have plenty of time
> for poetizing and dreaming there. What do you say to it?" I
> put on a little dignity; and though my heart was beating
> with delight I quietly thanked his Lordship. But when I
> had passed beyond the reach of episcopal vision, which is

Father P.A. Sheehan - Doneraile 1898
Courtesy Denis Madigan, Doneraile

far stretching enough, I spun my hat in the air and shouted like a schoolboy: Hurrah!.....

There was much work to be done in Doneraile, a large country parish. As well as the parish church in the village, there was also the Presentation Convent Chapel and a church in Shanballymore for attention. In a letter to Father Russell dated 29th August 1895, Father Sheehan said:

> ... I am afraid my second vocation must remain under-developed here for some time. This is a vast parish, somewhat neglected and run down, and there is a vast deal of uphill work before me. But, please God, all will come right in time. ......

It was some time before the people of Doneraile took to their new pastor. His apparent aloofness and manner of speaking, together with a degree of shyness and reticence placed a temporary barrier between him and his flock. It was a barrier that came down once the people got to know and understand the gentle and kindly man behind the facade and then both priest and people were united in a bond of friendship and co-operation that brought great benefits to the parish. He had come there towards the close of the Land War. There was much to be done as the Land Acts had cleared the way for tenant purchase and he was not found wanting with his help and advice to the tenant farmers.

He pressed on with his pastoral work, ably assisted by his curates. One of them was Father Timothy O'Callaghan, a man who had been very concerned with the land agitation problems. Born in Banteer, Co. Cork he had spent about ten years in the mission fields of Tasmania following his ordination, before returning home. He was a curate in Mallow when Father Sheehan was senior curate there and now they were together again in Doneraile. Father O'Callaghan was later transferred to Rathcormac where he died in 1903. A measure of the esteem in which he was held by both Rathcormac and Doneraile parishioners can be seen by the very impressive grave stone in the grounds of the Church of the Immaculate Conception in Rathcormac where he is buried. The inscription on the stone is as follows:-

"Timothy O'Callaghan C.C. Rathcormac died 25th June 1903 - 21st year of his sacred ministry aged 45 years. Erected by the parishioners of Rathcormac and Doneraile, by his numerous friends among the clergy and laity. In affectionate memory of a holy priest - the true friend and ardent lover of his country whose zeal for faith and fatherland hath consumed his energy at an early age."

Father Sheehan began to draw very close to his people in Doneraile. His great literary successes which will be discussed later would lead one to believe that he spent the greater part of his time in literary pursuits. This was not so as writing always was secondary to his sacred duties. Slowly but surely he began to get to grips with this very historic parish and as time went by the people began to see more clearly that here was a man who was their friend and to whom they could turn to in times of trouble and distress. They also saw a man who was eager to do what he could for his people both in a spiritual and temporal way and to improve the parish of Doneraile as a whole.

It was in the winter of 1900 that a major outbreak of fire occurred across the river from where his presbytery 'Bridge House' was located. It was in a saw mills where many local people were employed. Father Sheehan roused the villagers as very many of their houses had thatched roofs and were in extreme danger. Later he wrote:

> Something mysterious woke me from sleep as the clock was striking midnight. ... I rose and raised the blind. Across the river and not two hundred yards away the mill was on fire. Every coign and crevice was caught in the flames, which leaped through seventy windows and reared themselves thirty feet and above the roof. I could feel the heat in my bedroom, but could not hear a sound. Not a soul was stirring, although the single street was lighted as if by a hundred electric arcs. We could see great flakes of the fire falling on the convent roofs and lodging in the trees around . It seemed only a matter of minutes before the whole building would be wrapped in fire and smoke.

Luckily this did not happen and the nuns were roused and brought to safety. The mill was destroyed. Father Sheehan remained at the scene until the flames had subsided.

Although appearing austere in manner, the man behind the mask was quiet the opposite and could also see the lighter side of life. This comes through in a letter he wrote to a friend Sister Raphael in March 1901 regarding a wedding he attended.

I went to Limerick Junction the evening before and met a large party there. I had a comfortable room; but no sleep from the eternal rumbling of trains all night.. Next morning I started off and walked two mortal miles to a place called Solohead, hoping to be able to say Mass there. I found a fine church which you can see from the train; but alas! all the glory of the King's daughter was not from within. I found the church empty. There was a missal on the alter and a gorgeous tub of holy water in the middle of the floor. That was all. And it requires not much knowledge of rubics to know that you could not say Mass with these. Mrs. Darcy was nowhere to be found. So I had to walk back again 2 miles in a sour temper but in hopes that S. Joseph wouldn't blame me. Then a long journey of 10 miles in a close carriage. ... The guests were all assembled; and a particularly nice class the Limerick people are. Nice, refined and simple with not a trace of that stuckuppishness you find in the Corkonians. Then the cermony, during which the bride-groom pronounced his vows like a colonel commanding a regiment and the poor little bride broke down. Then congratulations and a meal just like a convent profession breakfast, speeches etc. and we started back for the Junction amid showers of rice, which I haven't got out of my hair as yet. ......

The Mrs. Darcy referred to in the letter is the famous fictional chapel woman in *My New Curate*.

Father Sheehan celebrated weekly Mass in Doneraile at 8 a.m. then made his thanksgiving and returned home for breakfast and read his post. A keen walker, he invariably took one in the morning into the country where he would often meet local people. It was from them no doubt that he gathered much of what he wrote in his books. When he returned from his walk he would write until around noon and then visit one or other of the schools. He didn't have his main meal until four thirty pm and so handled parochial administration before that. Each evening he would spend between 7 and 8 p.m. praying before the Blessed

Sacrament. Following his supper, he wrote until about ten p.m. when he would retire to bed. On Sundays he celebrated the early Mass and he invariably returned at 11.30 and was in the church when the second Mass was being celebrated. When this was over he held Sunday School for the children.

The early years of his ministry in Doneraile coincided with the closing stages of the Land War and the introduction of the Land Acts. During that time, the men of the parish met with him on Sundays at two o'clock in the Christian Brothers School and the tenant farmers hopes of ownership of their land was very much the main topic. In fact, Father Sheehan played a major part in the land negotiations between the landlords and the tenant farmers in Doneraile. He was the ideal man for such an undertaking, he was trustworthy with great integrity and above all else he was looked up to, not alone by this own people, but by those who were not of his persuasion. He was completely successful in bringing all the land negotiations he undertook in Doneraile to a successful conclusion.

There is conclusive evidence of this in surviving correspondence. Following his death, a very good friend, Mr. W. H. Grattan Flood of Enniscorthy was requested by Fr. Heuser in America who was then preparing a biography to forward any data he could get on the Doneraile Pastor's involvement with the land settlements in the parish of Doneraile. Mr. Flood contacted the Superior of the Christian Brothers School there, Brother P.A. Mulhall.

In a letter to Mr. Flood dated 22nd November 1913, Brother Mulhall enclosed a record of one of the tenants in Doneraile parish, Mr. J. O'Leary of Carrigeen written in indelible pencil. In that letter to Mr. Flood, Brother Mulhall wrote:

> *I enclose you particulars re the Doneraile Land purchase with which Canon Sheehan was so closely identified. Kindly keep these records till done with them and return same as they have been entrusted to me by a very mutual friend of the Canon and mine. He is most anxious to preserve them always must carefully.*

Record of Mr. J. O'Leary re Land Purchase in the Parish of Doneraile.

In the year 1903 the Wyndham Act was passed, and immediately the tenant farmers of the parish of Doneraile took steps to become the owners of their homes, as soon as ever they could. The first step taken in every case was to approach the parish priest, Canon Sheehan in whom they had a sympathetic and powerful advocate, whose voice and pen was always at their command.

The first estate in the parish to be sold was the property of Mr. J. W. Evans at Carker, in the year 1904. The Canon admitted to me that Evans had the best of that deal as the Canon at that time knew very little about land value. with his highly cultivated mind however it did not take him long to get a grasp of the facts. After that first sale he knew everything that was to be known about land purchase. The reason why this property was the dearest was because the holdings were in most cases small and the land with the exception of one or two farms was poor.

The second estate to be sold in the parish was the Crone property at Richardstown. The tenants on this estate became the owners of their homes at twenty one and half years purchase. This land is the best in the parish; and was always highly rented but through the united efforts of Canon Sheehan and the tenants the combination was effectual in making them happy and contented proprietors of the homes they were born in.

The third estate to be sold was that of Carrigeen and Rossa, known as the Creagh property. It is in this case I can speak with the greatest knowledge as I was closely connected with every phase in the negotiations.

In the year 1904 a few of the tenants put our heads together and decided to ask Canon Sheehan to come with us to meet our agent (A.G. Creagh of Mallow) in order to put before him our demand to purchase our farms. Twelve o'clock was the hour when the agent was to arrive in Doneraile to receive his rents from his twenty one serfs.

He was there punctually; so was Canon Sheehan. I shall never forget that hour, twelve o'clock on the 17 of September 1904 when Canon Sheehan cut the first link of that chain which had bound generations of tenants on the Creagh estate to the chariot of landlordism. The agent A.G. Creagh was represented by his son. The latter seemed very much surprised to see the dignified Canon leading his tenants into the room and to hear him in a few well chosen words put the case of the tenants before young Creagh. Mr. Creagh in a markedly insulting manner replied that Colonel Creagh was disposed to sell his property sometime but that he would not be dictated to by anyone, lay or clerical. The Canon left the room without much cermony and I accompanied him. At that moment I swore on oath that I would never pay another penny rent to Creagh, come what may, as long as I lived. So it was for two years and a half that I and another young tenant named Casey payed no rent to either agent or landlord, although we were threatened with the penalty of the law. We knew that we had behind us a power in the person of our distinguished parish priest Canon Sheehan. When threat of every description failed, Mr. Dudley, solicitor to the estate sent for me to see what could be done to open negotiations with the tenants. My answer to him was that, as the negotiations had been opened through Canon Sheehan on the first day, they must be reopened through him now. The rest of the story is soon told. A meeting of the tenants was convened by Canon Sheehan, at which the solicitor for the landlord was present. After some little give and take we purchased our farms at twenty and a half years purchase, or 6sh. 9d. in the pound on the existing rents. All arrears (and these amounted to a considerable sum) were to be wiped out. It was on 14 July 1907 that the first agreements were signed. During all these years Canon Sheehan had been our guiding star. The wisdom of his counsel I shall ever treasure and it was ready at all times, any hour, night or day. May his saintly spirit ever watch over the parish where his remains lie, is the prayer of J. O'Leary.

The fourth property was a tract of land owned by Saunders. The land was poor and the holdings mostly small; but the landlord was one of the worst of his class. Through Canon

Sheehan's exertions the tenants kept solidly together and by dint of organised action succeeded in bringing Saunders to sell the holdings at eighteen years purchase. It was the cheapest land deal in the district, with a considerable amount of arrears thrown off. By this purchase the Canon procured contentment and happiness in a large tract of his parish where heretofore there had been trouble with baliffs and sheriffs endeavouring to collect impossible rents.

The fifth property of which the Canon procured the sale by his intervention and advice was that of the Hills of Kilcoleman. It was transferred to the tenants at twenty years purchase on second term rents, with all arrears thrown off. Thus all the people of the Doneraile parish for the first time in centuries found themselves making their own homes and a prospect of peace and prosperity for their children. And it is to Canon Sheehan we owe it chiefly; for he was ever bent on up-holding the best traditions of our race and as a priest watched no less over the material than over the spiritual welfare of his people.

Following the satisfactory conclusion of the land purchases, he used his influence in getting as many improvements as possible for Doneraile. He was instrumental in getting an electric plant to provide light for the town and Doneraile Court. The power plant also supplied electricity to pump water to the houses which was an enormous benefit. Lord and Lady Castletown were very much his supporters in all this.

CHAPTER SIX

In the year 1904. Father Sheehan was awarded an Honorary Doctorate of Divinity by the Pope and the Bishop of Cloyne, Dr. Browne promoted him to Canon. That same year, because of pressure of work, he was advised to take a holiday and he chose to go to Germany. He had considerable admiration for the country and its people, especially with regard to their educational methods. Also of course, Germany was one of the first countries to appreciate his own literary work. The holiday was of considerable benefit to him but although he was to live until 1913, he was beginning to feel the effects of the serious illness that would later encompass him. This was evidenced from a letter he wrote to Dr. Heuser in America on the 7th June of the following year 1905 in which he said:

> *I have assigned to my Bishop and trustees all my literary property including GLENANAAR for the support of the sick and aged priests of this diocese. .....*

Because of the reputation Canon Sheehan had made in America through the success of his book *MY NEW CURATE*, it was felt at home that perhaps some advantage could be gained from it. A proposal was put to him that he would travel to America and endeavour to raise funds for the Cathedral in Cobh. His American friends advised him against it and at any rate, his precarious state of health did not encourage such an arduous undertaking. He declined the proposal.

The most influential people in Doneraile during Canon Sheehan's time there were Lord and Lady Castletown of Doneraile Court. Lady Castletown's family, the St. Legers had lived there for hundreds of years. They held the Canon in the highest regard and this made any negotiations he found necessary to undertake with them on behalf of his parishioners very amicable..

Lord Castletown (Sir Bernard Edward Barnaby Fitzpatrick) came from Upper Ossory and was member of a family whose Irish lineage went back to the early 1500s. The Castletown Coat of Arms had its motto in Irish - 'Ceart, Láidir, Abu.' (Might and Right for Ever). He had a very distinguished career. Born in 1849, he took a B.A. degree at Oxford and was MP for Portarlington 1880-83. He served with distinction in the

British Army in the late 1800s and served as Chancellor of the Royal University of Ireland 1906-09. In 1874 he married the Hon. Ursula Clare Emily St. Leger of Doneraile Court who was the only daughter of the 4th Viscount Doneraile who thus became Lady Castletown. Lord Castletown was involved in founding the Lawn Tennis and Croquet Clubs in Doneraile in 1910 and the Golf Club in 1912.

Canon Sheehan's success as a writer had turned him into a celebrity and whenever the Castletowns had guests of note, they were invariably brought to meet the man of letters. It was through them that the Canon met a very famous American for the first time in 1903. He was Justice Oliver Wendell Holmes and it was a meeting of two intellectual minds. They became close friends and engaged in a ten year correspondence which only ended at the Canon's death. The correspondence will be looked at later.

The Doneraile Pastor was very attentive to the care not alone of his parishioners but also to the parish property such as schools and churches. He was not a man who constantly demanded money and if and when he did seek help in that regard, the people knew that it was very necessary for him to do so. The church choir too always took his interest and this actually went back to his school days in Mallow when Father Patrick Horgan took him under his wing in the local church choir. During the Canon's time in Doneraile the parish choir was reputed to be one of the best in the south of Ireland and every Christmas he gave the choir members a supper over which he presided. This was followed by music, song and dancing and the Canon himself would invariably contribute to the singing. *The West's Asleep* and *A Nation Once Again* were among his favourites.

Christmas and Easter were scenes of great liturgical celebrations in Doneraile. During the Lenten devotions, very large crowds attended Rosary, Sermon and Benediction in the Church. The Passion Sermon on Good Friday night was the high-light of all the cermonies. It was not unusual for non Catholics to be present to hear the sermon and it was well known that many of the lukewarm Catholics, who seldom if ever attended Mass, were invariably present for that occasion. Recalling that Passion Sermon in his writing, Canon Sheehan had this to say:

> Men go to hear the Passion sermon who won't go to Mass.
> Protestants attend. The priest is chosen for the office as far

back as Ash Wednesday and if he is young and had not yet learned that the breadth of popular applause called fame is a very futile and fugitive thing, he is naturally nervous and apprehensive. The lines of the sermon too are strictly limited. It must extend to an hour at least. Anything short of that is a disappointment and it must follow detail after detail the gospel narrative. Any departure from that is viewed with great displeasure by the people and is gravely censured by the older priests. "'Twas a good sermon enough but 'twas not a Passion Sermon", that's the verdict.

Easter Sunday then was a day of liturgical festivity and joyful church music rang out during the celebration of High Mass. It was said that on one occasion a farmer from outside the parish of Doneraile having attended High Mass there for the first time remarked "'Twas aiqual to any two Masses I have ever heard before."

The Canon was noted for keeping a close check on his flock regarding attention to their religious duties and because of that it was not a regular feature of his ministry to have missions or retreats in the parish. A retreat was, however, held in the parish in 1912 and was conducted by a very close friend of his, Father Phelan S.J. The Canon's health by this time was failing but he assisted in every way possible including spending long hours hearing Confessions. One very elderly man commenting on the retreat said "These Missioners may as well stay at home as to be trying to bate the Canon in the Confessional or at the preaching aither - he's the best of the lot of 'em."

Canon Sheehan found wanting in Doneraile the stimulation engendered by good conversation and discussion. This he specifically referred to in a letter to Justice Oliver Wendel Holmes:

I felt my greatest want to be some intercourse with minds whose ideas would act as a stimulant to thought, by casting new lights on old subjects.

Yet despite that observation the Canon was an extremely humble man. Local recollections down through the years have testified to this.

As soon as he walked down the street the children would surround him, anxious to grip his hand or even a part of the cloak which he wore. On their way he would tell them stories and they in turn would tell him about school, home etc. They always had his interest. He was never impatient or sharp with them; it was not his nature to be like that.

He would visit the Convent school daily, where he spoke and joked with them. They loved him, loved to see him come, as lessons were set aside for the time being.

Mrs. Sophie O'Brien, wife of his great friend William O'Brien recalled:

The Presentation Sisters were great friends and admirers of their parish priest. It was pleasant to hear them tell all the good he did and how devoted to the instruction of the young. He would himself prepare little ones for first Communion. "The intellectual giant gives his time without stint to the humblest creatures" declared one of the nuns.

Again the Canon's great love of children is personified in his own writing:

I never go into a schoolroom without half-wishing, like John Bright, to shed a tear over those young lives with all the dread problems of life before them. Here, too, I think we should pour into these young lives all the wine and oil of gladness we may, consistently with the discipline that will fit them for the future struggle. I cannot bear to see a child weeping. I almost feel, like Cardinal Manning that 'every tear shed by a child is a blood-stain on the earth.' Yes, give them all the enjoyment they can hold. The struggle is before them.

Canon Sheehan not only loved children but also had a great understanding of them and their behaviour and of course their sense of humour. This was highlighted on an occasion when a little girl had been put outside the classroom door in the Convent School for mimicking the Canon's manner of speaking in front of the class. Canon Sheehan arrived shortly after the incident to find the child in tears. He brought her back into the classroom and was told that she had been imitating him. Smiling, the Canon said: "Now Mary, read a paragraph and let me hear how you can imitate me." This she did to the delight of the kindly priest and the children. He then shook the child's hand and said: "Not since my student days have I heard a better imitation of myself" and what started out for the child as a distressing matter ended up in laughter.

During Canon Sheehan's time in Doneraile, his cousin and great friend Mother Ita O'Connell was in the Presentation Convent there. As well as educational matters, he would discuss with her his literary ideas for books or articles and would bring her his manuscripts to read before sending them to publishers.

The Canon had a very close relationship with the Christian Brothers in Doneraile. They had been there since 1870 and had played a major role in the local boys' education. Throughout the main portion of his time as parish priest there, the Superior in the Brothers School was Brother P.A. Mulhall. He had come there just two years following his profession and remained there for almost thirty years. Towards the end of a long and very fruitful life in the field of education he recalled many very pleasant memories of the Canon:

> A phrase often used by Canon Sheehan was "boys will be boys". These words were also written in a letter he sent me a short time before he died. In that letter (it was quite possibly his last) the Canon asked me to use my influence to see that the boys would make less noise when playing near the parochial house which adjoined the school. The letter began "Boys will be boys" and expressed the hope that they would be less boisterous at play because of his great illness.The response to this appeal was remarkable. It was impressive to see the boys going tip-toe past the priest's house.

Brother Mulhall recalled how his friendship with the Canon began following his arrival in Doneraile and soon discovered how deeply he was interested in education. Before leaving for his new post, his Superior had said to him "You will have a good friend in Canon Sheehan if the schools are worked well".

> "You are welcome" was the Canon's greeting, "you can always look upon me as a friend." This he truly proved by his

47

extreme kindness and help to the Brothers in all their needs and by the great interest he took in the progress and welfare of the boys during their school days, as in after life. The kind and encouraging words that the Canon spoke to me on my arrival in Doneraile made us friends; this was the beginning of a close friendship which ended only with his death. In no instance was he ever wanting in his encouragement, support and kindly interest.

Local recollections too have recorded the quiet generosity of the Canon towards those in need:

> Canon Sheehan formed a branch of the St. Vincent de Paul Society in Doneraile and chose Mr. O'Callaghan as head of it. The help he gave to people that time is unknown. But many can tell of fathers dying when families were young and mothers left to care for five or six children and no Widow's Pension to help; the Canon befriended many such families. He would call to offer words of comfort to the grieving woman and by unobtrusive questioning learn of her financial position. Then secretly he would go to Mr. O'Callaghan's shop and order flour, sugar, tea and other necessary provisions for the family. Thus many people were saved from starvation through the generosity of their nameless friend - the human kindly Canon.

In June 1909, Bishop Jeremiah Doyle of the Diocese of Lismore in New South Wales, Australia died and Canon Sheehan was nominated as his replacement. It was a complete surprise to him when on the 17th July he received the congratulations of the priests of that diocese in the form of a cable. It was out of the question for him to accept the high honour, due to the poor state of his health.

In case pressure would be applied to him from Rome to accept the nomination, he contacted his very close friend Monsignor Keller of Youghal, then Vicar General of the Diocese of Cloyne and asked him to use his good offices through Cardinal Logue to allow his nomination be withdrawn. This was done and he was saved any further embarassment.

In September of the following year 1910 he consulted an eminent surgeon in Dublin named Sir Charles Ball who diagnosed cancer. In a letter to Fr. Heuser in America in December 1913. Mother Ita O'Connell of the Presentation Convent, Doneraile referred to this:

> ... *On 8th September 1910 he got his death warrant from one of the best Dublin Surgeons. He told me he received it as joyously as he would had it been an assurance of his perfect cure. He insisted on being told the exact state of his case - all the complications which may likely set in. The surgeon put everything before him and they were certainly enough to unnerve a stronger man but he took a brave view of everything. .... He often told me that he thanked God for giving him the Supreme grace of entire conformity to his holy will and that since he had heard his death sentence he had not one moment of depression throughout the long dreary days and sleepless nights. ....*

Apart from his brother Denis and one or two close friends, he kept the news a secret and continued with his parochial duties as before.

An illness such as Canon Sheehan had could not be kept secret for very long and tell tale signs became apparent both in his appearance and in his work. Soon it was public knowledge that the Canon was seriously ill. In 1912 he was confined to bed for some weeks and while he lay there the church bells of both the Catholic and Protestant communities remained silent lest the ailing priest be disturbed. Coupled with this, the roadway by his house was covered by tan bark to stifle the noise of carts passing by.

On the 22nd June 1912 Canon Sheehan was taken to the South Infirmary in Cork for treatment. Before he went to hospital he gave to Mother Ita O'Connell his favourite sister's Child of Mary large silver medal and told her to keep it always with her writing desk. Mother Ita did not know the sisters and was only a baby when they died but had heard all about them.

The acute pain that he was suffering lessened after some weeks and slowly he gained strength again. That early period in hospital was vividly described by him in a letter he wrote to a close friend on the 6th July.

I have been allowed up for a few hours yesterday and today and I take this opportunity of sending you the first buttetin of my progress twoards recovery. I say "progress" because I am very far from being out of the wood yet. I am astonishingly weak in physical strength and very emaciated but I suppose that will disappear. Not to speak of one or two daily experiences of what is meant by physical pain, I am having a life of luxurious idleness, for I cannot describe the attention and care of everyone here, from the matron down to the nurses, who do not know what to do for me. Their skill, their promptness and their solicitude are marvellous. The doctors are equally kind. Dr. Cremin has been watching me anxiously and Dr. Atkins is the kindest old gentleman in the world except when he hurts, when I draw in my breath and say: Suf. I have never said "damn" even once.

A good many people call but I cannot see them because my head aches from talking. Denis comes up every day for a couple of hours. I don't feel the time at all lonely except on a few occasions when I was in much agony. I lie down all day long, reading a little, praying a little - too little - and watching the wind tossing a big lime tree outside my window. But I look forward with a kind of terror to the future, beginning a weary life again and regretting, if it had been God's holy will, that I did not pass away.

No man was ever so eager to live as I was, and am to die. I think the wish is increased by the amount of human suffering I hear of here. ....

In a letter to Justice Oliver Wyndel Holmes in America he had this to say:

... I am pulling along like a bird with a broken wing: When Death looks in through one window, the doctors order him off, although I should like to open the door to him; and then he hovers around trying to get them off their guard. Some day he will succeed.

50

Further detail with regard to the Canon's illness can be found in the correspondence of Mother Ita O'Connell to Fr. Heuser.

... Towards the middle to June (1912) his life was despaired of and he was delighted that he was going so quickly. He was like a school boy looking forward to the home-coming. His Confessor used say he was the happiest and brightest patient he ever attended. The town and parish were full of gloom, he was the one happy person amongst us all. On the Feast of S. Heart nearly a hundred children offered their first H. Communion for his recovery and up to then he had refused point blank to see a second doctor, assuring everyone that nothing could be done for him and that he did not wish to live. However, prayer prevailed and he consented to have a second opinion and T.G. he got relief and was taken to Cork . .... His sufferings for the first six weeks were excruciating but he often told us the humiliating ordeals he had to submit to, were far more painful to him than the physical pain. .... He was threatened with terrible complications and one of the doctors was opposed to his leaving the hospital at all but when he found himself well enough to be up and about a bit, he began to pine for home .... He wrote me one day that he would "make a bold stroke for freedom" and was home to us in a fortnight.

Oh! the joy that news brought to his devoted flock. Bands, tar barrells, torches etc. etc. were in preparation, addresses and speeches were ready but when he heard it, he in his usual humility begged to be let slip home quietly. ..... When he was home for a few weeks and a little stronger we asked him to let them have their way and he consented, so the whole town and country were illuminated and the whole programme carried out much to his delight and he told us next day it was the greatest privation of his life not to have been able to address the people that night. .....

Canon Sheehan knew full well that his days were numbered. It was on the 25th November that he returned to Doneraile accompanied by a nurse and his brother Denis. Sitting in his favourite armchair he said to his housekeeper "I am home at last, thank God and nothing shall ever make me leave it again until I am in the coffin."

He struggled on with much of his parochial duties, though at times it must have been extremely difficult for him to do so. He heard Confessions and said Mass in the church. He survived the Winter of 1912 and also the Spring and Summer of the following year 1913. He was now getting extremely weak and as the Summer days drew to a close he began saying Mass in private. In fact on New Year's Day 1913 he had addressed the congregation at Mass and told them that before long he would have to leave them and said that he wished to be buried close to the church entrance. He apologised for his inability to carry out his duties as he should have done but ill health had prevented him from doing so. Many in the congregation wept openly at what he had said. "It is not want of will but want of strength that makes me fail in doing what I would for you, my dearest people" he said. He himself also broke down on this occasion.

He made his last visit to the Presentation Convent in Doneraile about two months before his death.

He wended his way, slowly and feebly, along the short cut by the bank of the River Awbeg (the "gentle Mulla") to the convent grounds - a distance of a few hundred yards. There he met the Reverend Mother and some of the Senior Sisters and went with them to their little summer-house where, in happier days, he had so often passed the community hour of recreation in their company. For the Sisters, the afternoon was overshadowed by a black cloud of sorrow. His greatly weakened condition filled them with grim foreboding. They knew that this was to be the final leave taking but no sign of anguished hearts was allowed to appear, no word or gesture that might upset their gentle guest and superior. They yearned to prolong the visit but feared he would not be able to stand the strain and when, after a short rest, he prepared to depart no attempt was made to detain him.

They went with him to the end of the path. All too soon the little gateway was reached. The parting time had come. The last farewells were said - only two words, "Goodbye, Canon", said gently and affectionately by each Sister and repeated as he turned to go.

Sadly and silently the little group of nuns watched his receding figure until, at a turn in the path, the projecting wall hid him from their view - for ever! They had hoped for one last sign, hoped that he would turn and wave a last farewell but they were disappointed. Canon Sheehan and his beloved Doneraile nuns had seen the last of each other this side of the grave.

Some of his personal effects are still in the Presentation Convent in Doneraile - a writing desk (this would appear to be his sister Hannah's), a prie dieu, a chessboard and some vestments. The nuns also hold autographed first editions of some of his books.

A short time before he died, he was in his study with his brother Denis. He took from his desk a bundle of papers - they were part of his autobiography. In a feeble voice he turned to his brother and said

"These might do harm to others, let us destroy them."

The papers were thrown on to the fire and in a short while were reduced to ashes.

It was of course a tragic loss to those who in the years ahead wished to study the great writer. William O'Brien on learning of it said that it was a noble act of self-denial. He felt that the Canon had been persecuted for his sympathy with the policy of the All-for-Ireland League. According to the O'Briens, the Canon while he was alive was reticent on the subject and avoided it even with his closest friends. At the same time he couldn't write his life story without dealing with his political views but fearing the harm or upset that might do, he chose the path of destroying his papers.

Canon Sheehan struggled on until he could no longer cope, having said his last Mass on the Feast of the Assumption, August 15th and on the evening of Rosary Sunday October 5th 1913 he died peacefully. He had already let it be known the inscription he wanted included on his headstone:

"Where Dwellest Thou, Rabbi?"

And Jesus said

"Come and See."

Mother Ita O'Connell referring to his death in a letter to Fr. Heuser wrote:

> ... *The night he died, his remains were brought down stairs and when laid out, the hall door was opened and the street outside was crowded with people and the little children rushed into the room to see their loved Canon. It was touching to see the babies settling the vestments on his bed. The poor people remained all night and next day he was removed to the Church. ... The two traits in the Canon's character which appealed most to his people were his great humility and his wonderful charity, both in word and in act. His purse was always open to the poor and he invariably suppressed his name and got the charity dispensed by another person. One of his last acts when he was almost unable to walk was to come here (to the Pres. Convent) to give £1 to a poor couple whom he had heard that day were in want.*

Canon Sheehan left no riches behind him and a copy of his will is shown here.

William O'Brien and his wife had been regular visitors to the Canon during the last months of his illness. Mrs. O'Brien recalling this many years later said that the Canon was too ill to leave the presbytery.

> He told us he could not pay us a visit, that we were to come and see him as often as we could manage it. Through that pleasant September weather we often drove to Mallow. Alas! as each week passed, we noticed he was growing weaker. He would not speak of his illness. We knew about it from his brother, who stayed with him and watched over him with the tenderness of a woman. The Mallow doctor who was devoted to the poor sufferer told us all he could do was to try and ease the pain. He often failed. He dreaded what

This is the Last Will and Testament of the Very Rev. Patrick Augustine Sheehan D.D. P.P. made on the 8th day of January, 1912. I appoint the Reverend Denis O'Connor. Adm. York Terrace, Queenstown, and Denis Bernard Sheehan, Local Government Auditor, Seafield, Queenstown, my Executors. I give and bequeath to the Treasurer of the Vincent de Paul Society, Mallow, the sum of Fifty Pounds (£50) for the poor of Mallow; and a similar sum of Fifty Pounds (£50) to the Treasurer of the Vincent de Paul Society, Doneraile for the poor of Doneraile. I bequeath the sum of Twenty Pounds (£20) to my Successor in the parish of Doneraile for the poor of Shanballymore. I bequeath to my Executors the sum of one hundred Pounds to be expended in Masses to be said for the repose of my soul in Churches open to the public; and I appoint my brother, Denis Bernard Sheehan my residuary Legatee, giving and bequeathing to him all else I shall die possessed of.

Signed by the said Testator as and for his Last Will and Testament in our presence, who in his presence, and in presence of each other, all being present at the same Time, have hereunto signed our names as Witnesses

Testator:

Patrick Augustine Sheehan

Witnesses:

Thomas Shinkwin
Stephen Wigmore

Dated at Doneraile, the 8th day of January. 1912.

the future might bring. Our last visit remains very vividly in my memory. He lay very white. His brother whispered the night had been very bad. My husband's presence seemed to revive him better than a cordial - he talked of his favourite topics. He would not let us go. William O'Brien expressed the fear that we might tire him. He insisted it did him good to see us. ... Next time we were driving along the road which had been so familiar, we met the doctor returning to Mallow. He stopped us and told us the patient could not see us. He had suffered a great deal and was now asleep. He added he was dreading the pain of the next few days. ... With heavy heart next day we went to Cork. My husband had to attend a meeting in the neighbourhood. He returned to Turner's Hotel late and worn out. We went to bed. A knock came to our door to tell us Canon Sheehan was dead.

CHAPTER SEVEN

Glowing tributes and memorable recollections were recorded following Canon Sheehan's death and from them we are able to gather much knowledge about the humble priest and yet famous author. Perhaps one of the finest of those tributes came from the pen of the late Mr. John J. Horgan earlier referred to.

> I remember very well the last occasion on which I visited him at Doneraile. It was a glorious Spring day .... I had come for the week-end, one of the many that I had the honour and privilege of spending under his roof. There was, as always, the kindly, hospitable welcome, the enquiries after many common friends, the discussion of events in the great world which here seemed so remote. In the afternoon we went for a drive to visit the historic Kilcolman where Spencer lived and wrote the *FAERIE QUEEN*. ... Back at Doneraile again, we spent the afternoon in the garden he loved so well. ... Here he showed me the crocuses bursting up joyously from their winter sleep and we paced up and down the narrow sheltered path where much of his work was thought out. There too was the little wooden summerhouse where, in Summer, he often wrote. ...
>
> He never shone in a crowd. His natural shyness and modesty, which he so often admitted and deplored, seemed in a crowded company to dry up that delightful easy flow of genial, speculative conversation to which those who knew him intimately loved to listen. But with a friend on a country walk or by his own fireside, few men were more interesting or more entertaining. : interesting not only because he talked well himself, but because, like all good talkers, he drew from his companion the best he could give to the common discussion. Americans and others anxious to meet the famous author often travelled to Doneraile to see him, but I fear many went away without ever meeting the real Canon Sheehan that his friends knew so well.

Referring to the reserved manner of Canon Sheehan, Fr. W. F. Browne, Bishop's Secretary wrote in 1914:

*... My intercourse with the Canon - apart from occasional
business correspondence - was practically confined to the
times when, with the Canons, he attended Chapter meetings
here (Queenstown). On such occasions, he was one of the most
silent and reserved of men. At dinner, he would hardly join in
the conversation at all, though I always thought of Burns
"There's a chiel amang us takin' notes." He was always
corteous and polite, of course, but very silent. ... I rather
thought that his silent reserved manner would have kept
people in awe of him, yet when he died all the older
generation had instances to relate of his unostentatious
kindness especially to the poor and sick.*

Mr. J. J. Horgan later wrote:

I came again to Doneraile on the day of his funeral. All the
countryside had come to do him homage. A nation mourned
by his grave. Lords and Members of Parliament, farmers and
labourers, professional men and artisans, all were at one in
their sorrow and in their loss. But it was in the little house
by the river that one missed him most. The gentle presence,
the quiet voice, the kindly smile, all gone.......

Lord Castletown, a close friend and admirer of the Canon keenly felt
his passing and said:

I have never ceased to grieve (since his death) for the
departure to his home of one who was my kindest counsellor
and intimate friend. He was, as one of the poor people said 'a
saint on earth' and I am sure he is now 'a saint in heaven'.

The late Mother Benignus of the Presentation Convent, Doneraile
remembered Canon Sheehan very well, having come to the convent
around the time that his health was beginning to deteriorate. She
recalled in a radio interview her memories of him:

"He came to the convent school every day and particularly at
the cathechism time and had chats in the infants school. He
spoke to all the infants. They gave him their secrets, always
to him and never to the nuns. He could get them to talk
without any effort - they poured out to him .. he was tall,

A floral tribute on Canon Sheehan's grave following his burial.
Courtesy Michael Shine, Doneraile.

thin, very stately. He wore what you'd call a cloak to his knees - one of the old fashioned cloaks you know on a wet day and when he came to the cross, the children would be going in under the cloak so that he could hardly walk.

The late John Walsh of Laharn referring on radio to his memories of Canon Sheehan recalled that the first time he met him was when his mother was very ill and the Canon came to see her. When asked if he was impressed by Canon Sheehan he replied

"I was of course. Anyone would be impressed by him. His sermons were marvellous altogether and the simplest person could understand them. You could hold listening to him on the coldest Winter's morning. You'd be enthralled. He made the remark once 'They say I have a proud walk'. Well, he used to walk very straight and he always wore a tall hat. He wasn't a proud man at all though a stranger might think he was. And I'll never forget as long as I live the last sermon he gave us when he went up in the pulpit to bid us goodbye. We knew he was dying too at the time. He knew it himself but it would make the stones cry to listen to him and his last goodbye. Well, I was very proud to be laying the wreath on his grave on the fiftieth anniversary of his death"

In recent times John O'Toole of Graigue, Shanballymore recalled memories of the late Canon Sheehan:

On one occasion when he came to say Mass in the old church in Shamballymore the altar boy didn't turn up and he asked me to serve Mass. I was young at the time and when Mass was over he said to me "get your father to buy you a donkey and come in to the Christian Brothers school in Doneraile." I never got the donkey. .... he was a good preacher, not too long - winded ... after returning from Germany he told the local people that Germany was preparing for war. He was great for chatting up old people, ... he was compassionate and good to the poor. There was a chemist named Jones in Doneraile, a Protestant man and he had a brother who was a writer and very friendly with the Canon. ... Jones was a Northern Ireland man. ... The Canon came out to Shanballymore in a side car, driven by a Doneraile man. He drove him everywhere he wanted to go. One of the curates in Doneraile that time was a Fr. Fizgibbon and he had a pony and trap. .... During the tenant farmer problems a labourer was getting a shilling a day, at harvest time a half crown. A man with a scythe would cut an acre of corn in a day. ... You know when Dr. Croke was parish p;riest of Doneraile, that would be now in the late 1860s, he asked Lord Doneraile for ground to build a Christian Brothers school and was refused. Croke said he'd build it at the rear of the Presbytery where there was space. He consulted my grandfather Patrick O'Toole who was a Poor Law Guardian. They started a fund to build a school and a Brothers' house. The grandfather started off the fund by giving five pounds, a lot of money that time and the school was built.

As was his wish, Canon Sheehan's grave is marked by a Celtic Cross. He hoped that people would not forget him but would pause on their way in and out of the church and pray for him. However, it was felt that it wasn't enough and soon after his death, the idea of a national monument to be located in the parish was mooted and a committee was set up to raise funds for such a project. Mallow was already thinking along the same lines.

At the outset there were a number of ideas as to what form the memorial would take, one being a chime of bells and another very much favoured was some type of charity for the aged and the poor. Brother P.A. Mulhall, Superior of the Christian Brothers in Doneraile and long time friend of the Canon's was the honorary secretary to the committee. At the end of November 1913 he wrote to Dr. Grattan Flood in Enniscorthy who was a very great friend of his own and that of the late Canon's seeking assistance in getting articles re the proposed Canon Sheehan Memorial published in influential Catholic papers both at home and abroad, especially in America and Germany. Although the committee hadn't been very long formed, they had at that time collected over £460 - a considerable sum. However, the Mallow Memorial Committee were also very active with the object of having the memorial sited in Mallow, the birthplace of Canon Sheehan. There was an immediate conflict of interests which was to the detriment of both committees. The Mallow committee wrote to Dr. Heuser pointing out it was Mallow that gave birth to the late Canon when he spent his youthful years and two terms as Curate.

Although the Doneraile National Monument Committee had been extremely active and their Hon. Secretary, Brother P.A. Mulhall had been in contact with Fr. Heuser, a great deal of behind the scene lobbying of the latter was undertaken by Mother Ita O'Connell to have the proposed monument erected in Doneraile and not in Mallow.

The surviving correspondence shows that she kept the American priest very well informed as to the progress being made in Doneraile with regard to fund raising and as to why she felt Doneraile should be the National Memorial site.

> ... I know full well the link between you and our much lamented Canon and I feel sure you would not turn a deaf ear to any appeal made to you which would tend to honour his memory in any way. I have often heard our dear Canon relate the incident which brought about the making of his fame and the part you played in it on that eventful occasion when you made him proceed with My New Curate. Your high appreciation of his works brightened many a sad hour and encouraged him to continue his writings not withstanding the great opposition he was getting at home. ... I daresay you have heard of the efforts being made here to erect a memorial to him. The Committee have been advised to ask you to receive the subscriptions forwarded to you. ... The Committee have nearly £500 on hands already. ...

The fact that the Mallow National Monument Committee were seeking support in America was the cause of grave concern in Doneraile. Mallow had a very strong case too as to why the memorial should be sited there and had many influential people pleading their case as can be seen from their circular. However, because of his long association with Canon Sheehan as an author, Fr. Heuser favoured Doneraile.

The then Bishop of Cloyne, Bishop Browne kept out of the controversy and made no public pronouncement that would influence the situation one way or another. However, in a letter to Fr. Heuser dated 31st December 1913 he said:

> ...As to the project of two Memorials to Canon Sheehan - one in Doneraile and another in Mallow ... I and very many

Canon Sheehan National Memorial Committee.
DONERAILE, CO. CORK,

2 5 . 1 0 . 191 7

REV. FATHER SHINKWIN, Chairman

DR. WM. SHEEHAN, Vice-Chairman.

P. J. O'BRIEN, Manager National Bank, Treasurer.

REV. BR. P. A. MULHALL, Hon. Secretary.

JOHN MURPHY, R.D.C., Chairman Mallow Board of Guardians, and

WILLIAM GALLAGHER, Assistant Secretaries.

COMMITTEE.

REV. FATHER REA, C.C.

PHILIP HAROLD BARRY, J.P.

EUSTACE MORROGH BERNARD.

DENIS MURPHY, C.P.S., F.A.I.

JOHN O'CONNOR, J.P.

TIMOTHY SHEEHAN.

MICHAEL MURPHY.

WILLIAM ROBERTS, Shanballymore.

MICHAEL O'CALLAGHAN.

*friends of the late Canon are opposed to the idea of having
two memorials to be erected by the public. They can but
destroy the hope of having one respectable and worthy
Monument - Mallow claims on the ground that Canon
Sheehan was born there - and Doneraile seems to me to have
a better claim in that Canon Sheehan was the parish priest -
that he elected to remain P.P. of Doneraile, when the Bishop
offered to advance him to more prominent parishes - that he
died in Doneraile and wished to be buried there, and perhaps
more especially in that he is known to the literary world as
"Canon Sheehan of Doneraile."*

*I had to disassociate myself from the prospect of a double
Monument or Memorial and so I have refused to allow my
name to appear on either Committee (Mallow or Doneraile)
or to subscribe in hope that they would come to an
understanding that there would be but one Memorial -
whether the place selected be Doneraile or Mallow. My own
opinion is that Doneraile has the better claim. ....*

Fr. Heuser forwarded his own subscription to Mother Ita for the
Doneraile project at the end of 1913. He was perturbed, however, at the
unfavourable impression being created in America with regard to the
activities of the two Committees and he wrote to Mother Ita
accordingly. In a reply to him dated 6th January 1914 she said:

*... Your news about the unfavourable impression which the
two appeals are making fretted us greatly but there is no help
for it now. For many of his (Canon Sheehan's) friends, the
division has taken all the good out of the grand effort made
to honour his memory. ... At the same time there is none of
that strife between them that people at a distance imagine.*

Mother Ita was concerned at the poor American response to date
towards the Doneraile Memorial but was happy with the way things
were going on the home front. By the end of January 1914, £600 had been
collected and in a letter to Father Heuser she remarked:

*... but they would want at least £1000 to put up something
fairly decent. We have great hope that it will be some
charity for the aged and suffering poor. The greater number*

PROPOSED NATIONAL MONUMENT

TO

Canon P. A. Sheehan, D.D.,

at his Birthplace, Mallow.

◆━◆◆◆━◆◆◆━◆◆◆━◆

President :
THE MOST REV. DR. MANNIX, *Coadjutor Archbishop of Melbourne.*

Vice-Presidents :
The Right Hon. Sir W. M. Johnson, Bart. ;
His Honor the Recorder of Cork ; William O'Brien, M.P. ; Sir Bertram C. A. Windle, President University, Cork ; Colonel J. Grove White, D.L. ; Kingsmill B. Williams, J.P. ; Right Hon. the Attorney General for Ireland ; The Hon. Judge William Sullivan, Boston, U.S.A. ; and Very Rev. Morgan M. Sheedy, LL.D., St. John's, Altoona, Pa., U.S.A.

Local Treasurers at Mallow :
James J. Dudley, John Moran, Major John Creagh, Edward Fitzgerald, James Nunan.

Hon. Secretaries at Mallow :
John A. O'Connell, Henry H. Hanley, Daniel Kepple, John Griffin.

Secretary :
William Fitzpatrick, Mallow.

◆━◆◆◆━◆◆◆━◆◆◆━◆

D ar

The great love and admiration for the works of the distinguished Novelist, Essayist and Poet Dr. P. A. Sheehan must ever endure. His place in literature has been long assured. His characteristics will be ever manifested in his charming books ; but it is felt that the pride of a Nation that bore so eminent a son should be publicly and enduringly manifested by the erection of a National Memorial. To this project it is believed admirers all the world over will subscribe, so that as is usual in all countries a public Monument in his native town will in some way proclaim the appreciation of his contemporaries, the admiration of his readers, and the love of those who were privileged to know him. May we therefore bring the project under your notice, and respectfully request that in the event of your deciding to subscribe, your subscription should be sent as early as possible to the Treasurers.

JOHN A. O'CONNELL,
HENRY H. HANLEY,   } *Hon. Secs.*
DANIEL KEPPLE,
JOHN GRIFFIN,

WILLIAM FITZPATRICK, Secretary, Mallow.

are in favour of this but others are clinging to a statue of him.
... the poor people say "we want to see him once more before
we die and we would like to have him for future generations
to look up to."....

An article appeared in the American Ecclesiastical Review early in
1914 regarding the National Monument to Canon Sheehan and it
favoured Doneraile. The Committee had it published in the Cork
papers. The advent of the First World War caused a lull both at home
and abroad with regard to the memorial. Many felt however that the
war would be over by Christmas 1914. This of course was not to be and
the war coupled with the uprising of 1916 placed a different complex on
many things. Although the National Memorial controversy decreased
in importance with the upheavels in the country, Doneraile was still
very much the favoured location. Controversy and debate did carry on
however as to what form the memorial should take. Well over £700
had eventually been collected by the Doneraile Committee and this
added to Fr. Heuser's money which he collected in America gave them
a firm base on which to go on. The committee were adamant that a
memorial would be sited in Doneraile and a statue of the late Canon
was the eventual choice.

At a meeting of the Memorial Committee on October 25th 1917 the
following resolution was proposed by Mr. J. Murphy and seconded by Mr.
J. J. O'Connor as follows:

"that any surplus over and above the £700 already reserved
for statue be devoted to the erection of a suitable memorial
within the precincts of the Parish Church."

It wasn't until 1925 that final agreement was reached whereby the
National Memorial to Canon Sheehan would be sited in Doneraile. It
would take the form of a bronze statue of the Canon sited in the
churchyard. The surplus money that the local committee had would go
to putting some stained glass windows to the memory of Canon Sheehan
in the parish church.

Three stained glass windows were fitted, the cost of one being met by
the Presentation Convent Sisters. Two beautiful stained glass windows
to his memory were also fitted by the people of his native Mallow in
St. Mary's Church. They are to the left and right at the rear of the

main altar. The inscription on the window on the left is "VERY REV. P.A. CANON SHEEHAN" and that at the right is "PRIEST, POET AND AUTHOR".

The life-size memorial figure was executed by an eminent Dublin sculptor named Francis Doyle-Jones. It was he, who in the following year 1926 created the bronze statue of the famous Mitchelstown born Land League priest Father Michael B. Kennedy which is sited in the front grounds of the former Christian Brothers School in Fermoy and the sculptor was also responsible for the design of such momumental figures as Dr. Croke, John Redmond and John Mandeville and also the head of Michael Collins.

The pedestal supporting the statue was carved by Mr. N. Ellis, Monumental Works in Douglas St. Cork out of Little Island limestone. The statue was transported from Dublin to Mallow by rail, packed in a large crate. From Mallow, local Doneraile carrier James Cleary brought it by horse and cart to the Presentation Convent garden where it was kept for the night. On the following morning October 18th the statue was brought to the church grounds and placed on its pedestal. At noon on that fine October day, solemn High Mass was celebrated in the Church of the Nativity Doneraile by the Rev. F. M. Browne, S.J. and presided over by His Lordship Most Rev. Dr. Browne, Bishop of Cloyne. The Church was packed to capacity and immediately after the Mass the memorial was unveiled by his Lordship. An enormous crowd witnessed the unveiling cermony, many having come from Mallow, from Fermoy and also from Cobh where he served as curate. The village of Doneraile was tastefully decorated for the great occasion with banners and flags, the latter bearing inscriptions such as "To God and Country True"; "Loved in life and in death;" "His memory shall never fade", etc. As the cermony drew to a close, a wreath was laid at the base of the monument by Miss Shelia O'Sullivan, daughter of Mr. Martin O'Sullivan.

A glowing tribute was paid by Dr. Browne, Bishop of Cloyne to Canon Sheehan and he went on to say:

> I believe that the first thoughts of the people of Doneraile and surrounding country today is of Canon Sheehan the great priest. He was revered and loved by every section of his flock. ... To those of you who had a personal and intimate

acquaintance with Canon Sheehan I fancy that the first thoughts of him will be of the ideal Christian gentleman, so unassuming, so gentle, so self-effacing. Never, I believe, did one hear a boastful word from his lips, famous though he was and certainly never did anyone hear him utter a bitter, cutting or uncharitable word of another. Like his great Master, he was ever meek and humble of heart. ....

The oration was delivered by Rev. M. J. Phelan, S.J. On that day also Mallow Hurling and Football Clubs were well represented as were the Cork Catholic Young Men's Society and the Doneraile St. Vincent de Paul Society. When the unveiling cermony was over, the Greenmount brass and Reed Band under its conductor Mr. C. O'Shea played a selection of Irish Airs.

The memorial had an inscription on it both in English and Irish. The inscription in English is given overleaf:

ERECTED

by his sorrowing parishioners and his very

many friends and admirers at home

and abroad in affectionate remembrance of the

VERY REV. P. A. CANNON SHEEHAN P.P.

D.D. DONERAILE A.D. 1895-1913

A most saintly and devoted pastor who

loved especially the Little Children

and the Poor

an author of world-wide fame. The

moral of whose writing was the Glory

of God and the uplifting of his

fellowmen.

An ardent lover of his country and one of

the most gentle and amiable of men.

His memory will be ever fondly cherished

May he Rest in Peace - Amen

William O'Brien was asked by the Memorial Committee to speak on the occasion of the unveiling of the statue. He felt obliged to refuse. He advised the committee by letter as to his reason for doing so and went on to say:

I have long since given up public speaking. If anything should reconcile me to facing a popular audience again, it would be the privilege of saying a word of homage in memory of one of the most illustrious of my contemporaries and the most cherished of my friends.

Canon Sheehan's fame is, however, now enthroned too high to be greatly magnified by the voice of praise and it can never be hurt again by any whisper of disparagement. ...

Commeration of 50th Anniversary of the death of Canon P. A. Sheehan at his grave in Doneraile October 1963. Standing L to R: John Walsh, Laharn, Doneraile; Sergeant Geary Doneraile; Maurice Meade N.T. Skehanagh, Doneraile

It was while Canon Sheehan was stationed in Cobh that he began to write seriously. He he also wrote childrens' stories. One of the earliest of those stories for children was called "Topsy" written for a children's magazine. Topsy was actually the name of a dog Canon Sheehan had as a pet and in a letter to Fr. Heuser from Mother Ita O'Connell we get to learn a great deal about it.

> ... *He often told us about him, he could almost read his thoughts. When the Canon was leaving Exeter, he took Topsy about 20 or 30 miles by train to a young priest whom he could rely on to care him well as he could not bring him to Ireland not having a home there and doubtful as to his future mission. He felt intensely lonely after Topsy. About a week after parting with him, he was sitting at his window and to his amazement there was poor Topsy making his way very slowly towards the house, tired and hungry after his walk of over twenty miles on by the railway. The Canon had a letter the following morning from the priest saying Topsy had disappeared and for the week had taken very little food but was constantly crying and searching for his master. Notwithstanding his grief, he took him by force to the guard of the train next day to take him back to the priest but no coaxing would stir him from the Canon. As a last resource the guard told the Canon to step into the carriage and in jumped poor Topsy after him. The Canon immediately jumped out again and closed the door on Topsy. He assured us, until a very late hour that night he could not sleep, he was so ashamed of himself and so full of remorse for practicing deceit on poor Topsy and he never got over the intense regret. He said it was his first and last deceitful act. He cried for hours and made a resolution that he would never again keep a dog lest he would get as attached to it as Topsy. ...*

Many of the early stories by Canon Sheehan were later reprinted by the Catholic Truth Society.

Because of the influence many authors achieved by their writings, Canon Sheehan saw very clearly that perhaps he too could exercise some influence over the lives of the people he wished to serve and so augment the spoken word from the pulpit.

In September 1881, his article entitled 'Religious Instruction in Intermediate Schools' appeared in a very reputable publication, *The Irish Ecclesiastical Record.* It was of great concern to him that religion in schools be put on a sound footing so that on leaving, young boys and girls would have their faith built on a firm basis.

As a comparative newcomer to having his work appear in public, he was very sensitive to criticism and he would not allow his full name on the article, just his initials. He was hoping that many of his fellow priests would read what he had written and perhaps take heed of it and react accordingly. To his disappointment, the article was more or less ignored. It was a set back but he pressed on and tackled other issues of concern to the church at that time. Foremost among them was the problem of emigration. He had first hand knowledge of it in Cobh, one of the main Irish ports of emigration and he wrote a comprehensive article entitled "The Effect of Emigration on the Irish Church". It appeared in *The Irish Ecclesiastical Record* in October 1882 and this time it was signed P.A. Sheehan. It was a plea from the heart to both laity and clergy to be aware of and come alive to the various forces which appeared to be renewing the mass emigration of the 1850s and to the havoc being wrought on the Irish Catholic church.

Despite the great exodus after the Famine, about three million in thirty years, it was felt by many in authority that Ireland was still over populated. Early in his article Canon Sheehan drew attention to this:

> ... A bill has just passed through Parliament for advancing State aid to assist emigration; private speculators, very active with circumscribed limits are carrying out the new experiment; it is urged on and warmly recommended by leader writers and pamphleteers. ... Now how does all this affect us, Irish priests? How does it affect the Church with which we are so closely identified. ... We have no desire to import the angry elements of political strife into the calm pages of a theological journal. We simply wish to show the effect on the Church of this terrible drain on the strength of the country. ...

Let us come back to the present (1882). During the last three years, emigration that might be almost said to have ceased has set in, in a full strong tide that reminds us of the panic of the famine years. During the first four months of this year 39,000 Irish people passed through this port of Queenstown *en route* to America; and I think we shall not exaggerate when we state that during the same period, at least 10,000 left for America or England through Londonderry, Limerick, Galway and Dublin. This is a total of 50,000. During the same months of the present year or rather during the first quarter, 7,000 peasants were evicted without being reinstated as caretakers and during the second quarter that number increased to 11,000. ... Again, we are not exaggerating in stating the number of evicted person this year as 50,000. ...

That was the scene Canon Sheehan painted in 1882. He took issue with those who created such conditions and challenged those at home to do something more than support Bills in the English House of Commons which encouraged and supported emigration.

... whilst America is beckoning and leading, friends at home are pushing and driving the Irish peasant in the same direction. ....

It was a difficult message to hammer home to those intent on leaving. Little blame could be placed at the feet of the thousands of Irish boys and girls who were going to the New World, many through the support of those in their families who had gone before them and had made good. For them to be asked to remain in Ireland would be akin to the old saying "Live horse and you'll eat grass."

Canon Sheehan was being mindful too of the position the Catholic Church was finding itself in:

... If this state of things continues, in less than ten years, the ancient ecclesiastical divisions of Ireland will be obliterated and parishes amalgamated with parishes. ... Again let us not expect prosperity for our people so long as they are dependent on the agricultural resources of the country. Employment must be created for the surplus population of town and country by the establishment and development of local industries. The 'whirr of the wheel', the 'gliding of shuttles', the 'ringing of steel' must be the Resurrection March of our people. ...

The essay did not draw much attention.

While in Cobh too, especially in his early years there, he wrote some serious articles on diverse subjects such as one on *'Gambetta'*, the noted French republican, politician and liberal thinker, one on Emerson, the noted American writer who had died in 1882 and there were three essays on 'Education at German Universities' which the *Irish Ecclesiastical Record* published between June and August 1886. They were written as a type of blue print which he felt the Irish Universities should follow. On that subject he had this to say:

> ... University education in this modern world is supposed to have reached its most perfect form in Germany; and to Germany we must go to understand fully what appears to be the highest conception of University life, its spheres of thought limited only by the boundary lines of human knowledge and its work, free and flexible within rigid principles of religion on the one hand and patriotism on the other. ....

Canon Sheehan's ideas and criticisms of the educational system in Ireland were often opposed and resented as shall be seen later, especially by many of his clerical colleagues. He took issue with the fact that the system was calculated to train rather a body of anchorites and ascetics whose spiritual aims were too far removed from the actualities of life.

Despite the fact that he had the greatest admiration for both the German educational system and their literature, he wasn't blind to their military aspirations.

From an early age he had a great interest in St. Augustine and made an in-depth study of his life. The *Irish Ecclesiastical Record* had been a main source of publication for his work although in 1883 his writing attracted the attention of a Dublin Jesuit, Father Matthew Russell, editor of a magazine called *The Irish Monthly*. He was later to become a close friend and literary adviser to the Canon.

His return to Mallow marked the beginning of a new phase in his literary output. What had been up to then, by and large, an intellectual approach to writing through essays, literary criticisms and reviews was now augmented by the use of the pen as a means of spreading Christ's message on a broader canvas through short stories, poems and novels. Through these media, he hoped, not alone to entertain but to highlight what was both good and bad in Irish society and sow the seed for change.

In Mallow he began gathering material which was later to be the basis for his first book. His friendship with Fr. Matthew Russell deepened and among the contributions which the editor of *The Irish Monthly* received from him and published in January 1891 was an essay 'Irish Youth and High Ideals'. This actually had been the text of Canon Sheehan's inaugural address to the Literary Society he had formed in Mallow during his first curacy there.

The on-going clash between Sheehan the priest and Sheehan the author is highlighted here in a letter he wrote to Fr. Russell in January 1891 following the acceptance of his essay.

> ... *You have the charity of an archangel. I never dreamt of seeing my lecture in print again. I sent it simply for your amusement. It is only my implicit trust in the same charity that has tempted me to disinter the enclosed papers written in Maynooth under the Presidency of your distinguished uncle. I have found them in an old note book, and sent them just as they were written. I am afraid to look them over with a view to correcting them, lest I should put them in the grave of many ambitious efforts of mine - the fire. I sacrficed 200 pages of a story on the 8th December last because on reading them over I thought them of too secular a nature to put them in print. So I gave them to our Blessed Lady: but it cost me some trouble. I can only beg that you will "cut, burn and destroy" enclosed if you see in them anything faulty.*

Over the years, the fire claimed many manuscripts of Canon Sheehan, work that perhaps would have told us much to help us understand this clerical writer.

Poetry too was of great interest to him and he made a deep study of the great poets of his day. He also wrote a considerable amount of poetry mostly with a religious theme.

Before he left Mallow he was completing a MS called *Geoffrey Austin, Student* which was to become his first novel. He was also engaged in a sequel to it called *The Triumph Of Failure* and the third was a MS later to be given the title *My New Curate*. He also mentioned to Fr. Russell that he had a collection of sermons and essays dealing with the Blessed Virgin which he hoped one day may be published.

Perhaps some day I may see these little meditations in book form and be able to assure myself that I have done something for God before I die. Nearly all these sermons were written in England. ...

They were later published in book form under the title *Mariae Corona*. He was also working on ther projects:

The first a school tale in which I shall try and develop all my own hobbies; the 2nd A tale of the South Coast - a reproduction on a religious basis of the novel I burned three years ago; and 3rd, partly written "The Work and Wants of an Irish Church" which if ever I complete it, will be an important work. ....

The schooltale and *A Tale of the South Coast* were never published, whether he had ever completed them in MS form is open to conjecture. *The Work and Wants of the Irish Church* never appears to have been completed. His early biographer, Dr. Heuser found part of it among his papers. It showed his views on clerical education.

CHAPTER NINE

Canon Sheehan: MS *Geoffry Austin Student* was accepted for publication by Messrs M.H. Gill, Dublin and he dedicated it *"To the Catholic Youth of Ireland in whose future our highest interests are involved."* It was a book he was very proud of and of course it was his first big step into the literary world, a step he knew would be fraught with criticism from many quarters that would often bring hurt, disappointment and sadness. To alleviate some of this, he arranged that the book he brought out without his name. It was published towards the end of 1895. From a sales point of view it was not very successful at the outset. The book was, to an extent, a series of stories with a unifying thread running through it but had little in the way of a plot.

It was set in a Dublin Secondary College and in it the author sought to highlight the necessity of a sound moral and religious training in the field of education as a prerequisite for any fulfilment in life's achievements and that without Christianity life was lacking an essential ingredient. The book was critical of the inadequate religious instruction then existing in Irish Education. The character Geoffrey Austin was shown as drifting like a ship without the rudder of sound Christian teaching to guide him. The book was an academic exercise which showed the scholarly side of its anonymous author and the characters did not really come to life. Maynooth certainly didn't enthuse over the book. It was well received in Germany and also in some of the Catholic Journals in America such as *The Catholic World* in New York . It did attract the notice of Irish critics who, on the whole, conceded that it had literary merit. Displeasure however was expressed at the author's implied criticism of the Catholic education system. The strongest criticisms came from the Catholic clergy and Canon Sheehan was hurt by them, even though his name was not on the book as author.

He was disappointed at its reception but nevertheless some reviews were encouraging and it was one such review that helped put him on the road to fame. It appeared in a prestigious Catholic American magazine called *The Ecclesiastical Review.* Its editor was of German descent. Fr. Herman Heuser D.D. Apart from the review itself, Fr. Heuser was very interested in learning more about the anonymous author of *Geoffrey Austin, Student.* Fr. Heuser was a professor attached to the St. Charles Borromeo Seminary, at Overbrook, Philadelphia since 1876 and was actually in Ireland during the Summer of 1897. He spent a few days in Dublin at the Gresham Hotel and on the 19th July wrote to Canon Sheehan in Doneraile saying that he had read with pleasure his book and asked if he would write some articles for his American magazine.

This was the breakthrough that Canon Sheehan wanted and he told Fr. Heuser that he had been anxious to communicate with the American priesthood.

> *I have been engaged for some time in putting together some ideas about clerical education. I have struck out the chapters and designs: and have written the first three chapters.*

He sent Fr. Heuser a layout of what he had planned. The material dealt with the decline in both faith and morals of the people, especially in the towns and cities which was being accentuated, he felt, by the rapidly changing times and outside influences. He was hoping and urging the Irish clergy to play their part in counteracting any disturbing influences and had written:

> *It is a question whether the Catholic Church in Ireland is quite prepared to meet the new phases which every day will become more pronounced and defined.*

It was a time of challenge and a time for change. Canon Sheehan was looking to the Irish clergy for a new leadership. New thinking and new forms of clerical education and training were necessary, he felt, if the tide was to be stemmed.

The material that he was planning and some of which he had written was not however what Fr. Heuser required at that time due to the fact that his magazine *The American Ecclesiastical Review* was then running a series in a somewhat similar vein and he wrote to Canon Sheehan saying:

> *I should prefer to make selection of some of the topics which are treated in isolated chapters of your proposed volume - any or all of which would be suitable matter for the current*

numbers of our magazine. In case you agree, let me have ten papers ... that you will send us one (or more) articles every two months, you to receive two hundred and fifty dollars (in ten or less frequent instalments) according to the receipt of the papers.

Because of the poor showing of Canon Sheehan's first novel, the publishers Messrs. Gill of Dublin were not interested in publishing his second book *The Triumph Of Failure*. It was a big disappointment but he pressed on. However, luck began to favour him with the arrival of a letter from Fr. Heuser dated March 15th 1898. The letter was to be a watershed in so far as the literary career of the Doneraile Parish Priest was concerned, affording him an entre to an American readership that otherwise he would never have got. The letter also laid the foundation for an association and friendship between the two priests that remained up to Canon Sheehan's death. In his letter Fr. Heuser said:

Last year I proposed to you to write some papers on Clerical training. Not hearing from you and seeing in the meantime some articles in a lighter vein, over your name, I concluded that you had abandoned the project of the series; and since I have material from writers here on the same subject, I am satisfied.

But I can make another to you, if agreeable. We want a series of papers entitled "Types of Catholic Priest": "My Pastors": My Curates" etc. These are to be sketches of character and priestly life, written in a mingled vein of humor and serious thought. Where they happen to point out any weak phases, it should be done in a way which could not possibly wound though it might suggest correction. If you do not find such writing to your taste, could you suggest to us someone who possesses the talent to portray men and describe their doings in the parish, in the home of the priest, the church, etc.; in company with other priests, etc.

It was an offer that Canon Sheehan couldn't afford to let pass. In fact he had much of the background already prepared and he replied accordingly.

It was just the material that Fr. Heuser was looking for and he began arrangements to have it serialised in the *Ecclesiastical Review* as soon as possible. He felt that the title of the series should be changed from *"Stray Leaves from an Irish Parish Priest's Diary"* to *"My New Curate"*. Canon Sheehan still wished to remain the anonymous author of the series. He was delighted that his MS would be serialised in such a prestigious journal which reached out to a large American readership.

The serialisation of *My New Curate* commenced in the May issue of the Ecclesiastical Review in 1898 and ran until September 1899. It proved to be extremely popular and placed its author firmly on the road to literary success. The story was set in a rural parish called Kilronan where the old parish priest, affectionately known as "Daddy Dan" together with his lethargic curate had allowed the parish to decline. The curate is eventually transferred and replaced by young Fr. Letheby who is full of new ideas and full of hope. The story had a two fold theme, that of the young priest's efforts to try and improve the lot of his people materially and also to try and put them back on the rails spiritually, where a carelessness and a laxness of religious fervour had taken over. The opposition, suspense and intrigue running through the story made it the author's best loved and most popular book. It was a light hearted story and yet it had hidden subleties that, although often comic, were very successful in getting a message home.

The character 'Daddy Dan' was excellently portrayed, a character which people in many parts of rural Ireland could relate to and could often identify with. Canon Sheehan said in a letter to Fr. Heuser at the end of May 1898:

> My great difficulty is to draw from life and yet avoid identifying any character with living persona. And we are so narrow and insular here in Ireland that it is almost impossible to prevent priests saying "That is so and so," "That is Father - " etc. But I shall steer clear, without wounding charity.

By and large, the reviews were kind and encouraging. There were, of course, some who didn't like the idea that certain defects among the Irish clergy should be paraded before the American public. Fr. Heuser kept the author informed as to how the serial was being received and sent him copies of the reviews.

To cement a relationship that was closely developing between the two priests, Canon Sheehan sent a photograph of himself to Fr. Heuser which he duly acknowledged.

> *Many thanks for the likeness of the author of "My New Curate" which gave me much pleasure. Being neither good looking or tall, I have never had the courage to have my photo taken, except in groups, behind somebody else; otherwise I should return the compliment.*

The success of the serialisation of *My New Curate* in America and among those at home who were readers of the *Ecclesiastical Review* ensured that there would not be any difficulty in having it accepted for publication in book form. Although the author remained anonymous, it didn't take very long to recognise who the writer was and he became the subject of much congratulations. The parish priest of Doneraile was becoming famous and many called to the Presbytery to see him including American, Canadian and Australian visitors to Ireland. *My New Curate* was even of great interest to Bishops as Fr. Matthew Russell pointed out in a letter to the author:

> *Dr. Keyes O'Dogherty, Bishop of Derry, was here yesterday. He told me that he had dined lately with the Bishop of Liverpool Dr. Whiteside, who spoke of "My New Curate" as the best written and most interesting thing of the day. Dr. O'Dogherty got all the numbers from some priest and then wrote to Dr. Whiteside that he agreed with him. The Bishop of Derry did not know it was you till I told him. A good omen for the Triumph of Failure.*

A trusted and valued friend of Canon Sheehan's since their school days in Mallow was William O'Brien and while on his way to Malta wrote to him saying:

> *The rewards of Irish authorship are not so numerous that one should be deprived of the pleasure of knowing how far the influence of your charming story has made itself felt.*

The success of *My New Curate* in America placed the author in a very strong position with regard to the viability of his second novel *The Triumph of Failure* which was still awaiting a publisher. In fact, Messrs. Burns and Oates, the London publishers brought out the book in November 1898, some six months after *My New Curate* began serialisation. It carried the name P.A. Sheehan as author and was priced at six shillings. Following the success of *My New Curate*, his first novel, *Geoffrey Austin Student* which up to then had very little commercial success now began to sell well.

CHAPTER TEN

It was a great thrill for Canon Sheehan to see his second novel *The Triumph Of Failure* in print with his name on its cover as author. Looking back many years later on those days, he related how he was brought down to earth very quickly one day in Dublin. He had gone into a bookshop and asked the young assistant if he could recommend some light Catholic literature. *Geoffrey Austin* was one the lad suggested. When the priest, endeavouring to keep a straight face, said that he had read it, the assistant quickly remarked: "There's *The Triumph Of Failure* Sir by the same author and between you and me it is a failure."

The *Triumph of Failure* attracted some favourable reviews but there were also many of an opposite point of view. The book was one of Canon Sheehan's own favourites and one in which he made full use of his literary talents to add weight to his priestly calling. The publishers sent out review copies to the journals and periodicals of the day including fifteen in America. Because of the success of the serialisation of *My New Curate*, the American market was being sought for the book. Canon Sheehan was happy enough with its reception in Ireland as we see from a letter he wrote to Fr. Heuser in America in early January 1899.

> *I am happy to say it is attracting some notice at this side. All the papers here have been very kind and extended articles will appear in the New Ireland Review, the Irish Ecclesiastical Record etc. Dr. William Barry of Dorchester, Oxford is taking it up warmly and is writing a long notice of it. But I look to America for the success of the book.*

Canon William Barry's review for the Catholic Times was very favourable and called on Irish and English readers to "read, mark, learn and invariably digest the moral of the book."

In a review by the *Irish Ecclesiastical Record* of *The Triumph Of Failure,* the opening paragraph had this to say:

> We are not certain how far this book will tend to lessen the deep-seated prejudice that very many people feel against the theological novel. To the ordinary novel reader, who seeks

amusement, or at best distraction from the stern and monotonous realities of life, the intrusion of solemn questions into a work of fiction may appear impertinent.

The New Ireland Review in its February issue of 1899 was in fact quite critical of the book. While conceding that the author was possessed of talent, the reviewer found many aspects of the book not to his liking and said:

> The plot scarcely deserves the name. It is a loose concentration of incidents, few of which are either new, or probable or well-developed. In the portrayal of character Father Sheehan has been equally or still more unsuccessful ... it is speculatively vague and it is practically unhelpful.

The success of *My New Curate* in serial form in America gave Canon Sheehan the confidence that he needed to keep on writing and he was very hopeful that it would be published in book form. Around the time the serialisation had come to an end in September 1899 Fr. Heuser was able to assure him about the book saying that there would be no difficulty finding a publisher. The Canon was very appreciative of the interest his American friend was taking in his work and in a letter said to him:

> *You have taken a great deal of trouble about my book and I cannot see that I can do better than leave the matter unreservedly in your hands. It would be quite impossible for me to form an opinion so far away from the centre of action.*

Fr. Heuser had a considerable amount of experience himself in publishing as editor of the *American Ecclesiastical Review* and was going to great pains to see that Canon Sheehan got the best deal possible. He was particularly concerned with regard to copyright of the material and felt that it would be better guarded by a reputable publisher than by himself. Accordingly, with the Canon's permission he negotiated the sale of the copyright of *My New Curate*. The author found this a most satisfactory arrangement to sell his copyright which was to prove advantageous to him in the years ahead, especially when the publishers Longmans were responsible for the publication of most of his books.

Longmans did not in fact publish *My New Curate* in book form. It was published late in 1899 in Boston by Marlier, Callanan & Co. whose London agents were Art & Book Co. The book was priced at six shillings.

The Irish Ecclesiastical Record in its Book Notices early in 1900 described *My New Curate* as of its kind "almost a perfect book" and went on to say:

> Indeed, the note of personal experience is felt all through the book. The ideal is held up to us in vivid light. ...We congratulate the author on the success he has achieved and on the honour that his work reflects on the priesthood of Ireland.

The *Irish Monthly* also in their issue of May 1990 carried a Book Notice of *My New Curate* saying:

> This thoroughly delightful volume, which is published in a very attractive form by a rising young firm in Boston, has at last reached our shores after keeping us waiting so long that already the book is in its fourth edition in the United States. We prophesy that it will be a record-breaking and epoch-making book. Though it is meant more directly for priests, it will do our own good lay-folk no harm to study, as they are sure to do.

My New Curate put Canon Sheehan on the road to literary fame and within a short time he became a household name both at home and abroad. He was very conscious of the great service the *American Ecclesiastical Review* had done him by serialisation. Accordingly, he wrote a preface for the book expressing his thanks to the American readers for their appreciation of his work in serial form. It did not arrive on time for the first edition of the book and was in fact never included.

The book had an easy passage through the review pages and the Doneraile parish priest became a celebrity, however much he wished not to. The parochial house was the focal point for many callers, some to congratulate and others to meet the famous author.

There was some criticism regarding the many similarities between *My New Curate* and that of the book *Diary of a Country Curate* by Monsignor Fonsegrive published some time previously. When asked about this by a friend, Sheehan replied:

> Yes, I know about that. Will you believe I had not ever seen Mons. Fonsegrive's book until long after "*My New Curate*" had appeared in print? However, I feel I may be sometimes guilty of plagiarism unconsciously, for I have a trecherous memory, though not in the usual sense.

An observation in a similar vein regarding *My New Curate* was made in a letter (undated) to Fr. Heuser following the appearance of an article on Canon Sheehan in the *American Ecclesiastical Review*. The letter was from the French translator of Sheehan's works, Fr. Joseph Bruneau S.S.

> ... the first extract of Canon Sheehan's work ever done into the French language was published by the Bulletin des Anciens Eleves de St Suplici and it was through the patronage of this splendid and inspiring periodical of the St. Suplice Alumini that the first volume "Mon Nouveau Vicaire" saw the light - being subscribed for in advance by those foreigners who, we are told, cannot be conscious of the racy Irish humour etc.
>
> The Letters of a Country Vicar by Yves le Querdec, Curate had something to do, I believe with Canon Sheehan's book. If it had not - which I very much doubt - it was a very strange coincidence and then surely a manifestation of the Qeitgeist that the same theme should be worked out in France and in Ireland, at such short distances.
>
> Though the literary merit of Yves le Querdec's book is far superior to that of My New Curate - any competent critic will agree - we who know what influence Mon Nouveau Vicaire had in inspiring French clerics with ambition for the saving of souls willingly and gratefully acknowledge our debt to the late Canon Sheehan.

My New Curate certainly made an impression on many of those who read it. Fr. W. F. Browne, Secretary to the Bishop of Cloyne in a letter to Fr. Heuser in January 1914 regarding the author wrote:

... One beautiful Sunday evening I came to a little fishing village, Port-en-bessin, about ten miles from Bayeux ... A priest from the neighbourhood enquired with the greatest interest about Canon Sheehan and told me that when the present Cardinal Amette of Paris was Bishop of Bayeux, he had the French translation of "My New Curate" read at recreation for the students of the Seminary there, and so deeply were they engrossed that the bell terminating each recreation was most unwelcome. ...

In the meantime Canon Sheehan was working on his fourth book called *Luke Delmege* and in the same year that *My New Curate* appeared in book form in Ireland, the year 1900, twenty four chapters of *Luke Delmege* were serialised in the *American Ecclesiastical Review.* It was the second of his clerical novels. An entry he made in a note book on 13th March 1901 said "I finished *Luke Delmege* this evening at 8 p.m. D.G.

Luke Delmege, a very long book of some 580 pages told the story of a priest Fr. Luke which began at the presentation of prizes in Maynooth at the end of his final year. He commences his priestly life with all the academic honours from Maynooth but he lacked the common touch and although meaning well, he was never really understood by the people he served.

The 24 chapters published in 1900 covered Luke's experiences on the English Mission. Fr. Heuser, decided to whet the appetites of his readers by leaving a gap of a few months following the publication of the first 24 chapters.

The second section of serialisation which dealt with Fr. Luke's return to Ireland and of his priestly life there then appeared. It was well received in America but the character Luke hadn't the same appeal as old Daddy Dan in *My New Curate* . Serialisation was completed in January 1902 and then it was then brought out in book form by Messrs. Longmans Green & Co. and priced six shillings.

Although there was considerable good will towards the book especially in America it aroused a great deal of controversy in Ireland

and drew down the wrath of many clerics because of its criticism of Maynooth's educational system.

Canon Sheehan's recollections of Maynooth weren't always complimentary.

I remember well that the impression made upon me by Maynooth College then and afterwards, when I saw its long, stone corridors, its immense bare, stony walls, the huge massive tables, etc. was one of rude Cyclopean strength, without any single aspect or feature of refinement. So too with its studies. ... The graces were nowhere. Even in the English Literature or Belles Lettres class, as it was called, the course seemed to be limited to hard grinding Latin and nothing more."

There was a great deal of Sheehan in the character Luke both on the English Mission and at home in Ireland. Following publication the critics had a field day and the author was stung by the very often hostile criticism. In a letter to his friend Fr. Russell he wrote:

"Yes! The Independent has been very vicious and unscrupulous. Exactly the same hand in exactly the same manner attacked "MY NEW CURATE' last year or 1900 in "United Irishman". There were the usual letters and - silence."

Referring to such criticism a year or so after Canon Sheehan died, Mother Ita O'Connell in a letter to Fr. Heuser said:

Many a sad hour your friendship lightened for our dear Canon in life. It is only of late I fully realise how hurt he often was by the unjust criticism. I used always try to convince him they were the outcome of jealousy and that he could afford to smile at them. ....

By now Canon Sheehan had suspected that many clerics were behind the critical onslaught, one or two being from the Diocese of Cloyne. One critic claimed that the Canon portrayed in Luke Delmege was created from a Canon in the Diocese although he was not prepared to put his name under what he wrote and signed himself "Mulla". The author, commenting on this to Fr. Russell said:

> "Mulla wasn't kind. It is absolutely untrue to say there is, or has been such a person as the Canon in this diocese. There is not one single character drawn from life but the Vicar General in England. The prototype there was old Herbert Woollett of Plymouth, dead about twenty years."

Canon Sheehan had served with Canon Woollett in Plymouth when the former had first arrived on the English Mission.

A very strong attack on the novel appeared in the form of a thirteen page article in the February 1902 issue of the *Irish Ecclesiastical Record* entitled *Luke Delmege* and signed J. F. Hogan, D.D. who later became President of Maynooth and had been a Professor of Modern Languages there. The article in its opening was congratulatory to the author but as one read on, one could feel the knife being very gently but firmly being driven home.

> The phases of clerical life with which it deals are touched by the hand of an expert. The humour and the pathos of the story will bring smiles and tears to many a fireside in Ireland and beyond the seas. ... The deep note of religious faith echoes through the book from beginning to end but the light note of humour tingles on the surface.

However, as the article progressed, Dr. Hogan began to hit home as he took his pen against the implied criticism of Maynooth.

> Maynooth, we observe, has come in for its share of the author's sly and pungent criticism; but Maynooth has withstood the shock of far more wicked assaults with comparative equanimity. ... The action of the story seems to us not to be well maintained. The connection of the various incidents with the main subject of the narrative and with one another is often involved in a sort of nebulous haze.

Slowly but surely, but always in the nicest way possible, Dr. Hogan dismembered the book, his final paragraph bringing the article to its ultimate intention.

The part of the work that is not religious will, on the other hand, have no more direct or practical effect than to interest and amuse the present generation and reflect to posterity the ways and manners of our time. And yet we are thankful, indeed, for what we have received. It is not perfect. It is not a classic. It is not a masterpiece. It is full of absurdities and of stilted nonsense. It is like a speech of Lord Roseberry, leaving us often times in doubt as to which side it takes. It is hopeless and helpless where both hope and help are needed. But in spite of these defects, and of others that we need not mention, it is, taking it all in all, a fascinating book, a clever, an instructive, and a good one.

It was extremely harsh criticism from a fellow priest. As a defender of Maynooth Dr. Hogan appears to have been over sensitive. No institution was perfect and Canon Sheehan as a novelist was using his craft to subtly highlight what he saw as possible defects. After all, by this time he had many years of experience in the pastoral work of a priest, experience that an academic such as Dr. Hogan probably lacked.

The author was deply hurt. He felt that Dr. Hogan did not at all get a true understanding of his book. Another author under such circumstances may have answered directly that criticism but it was not his style. In a letter to Fr. Russell, he commented:

> There is not much danger of being spoiled by these honours; but the delight of the poor people are everywhere. I am not quite so sure about the brethern.

What appeared to be of considerable annoyance to the author was the fact that following the serialisation of the first chapter of *Luke Delmege*, he had discussed his book with Dr. Hogan.

> I had a long conversation with Dr. Hogan of Maynooth about the motif and origin of the book. I explained that it was partly suggested by Fr. Yorke's structures on the College and that I designed to show that although a young student from Maynooth might be distinguished in College, he might easily be put to shame by flippant and foolish questions in the world; and that it would be well if the deep lessons of

scholastic philosophy were made advailable 'to the man in the street', or 'the man in the train.'

I told Dr. Hogan that I also wished to show that a young man's fancy might be caught by the glitter of modern literature; and how after many years and bitter experience, he might come to see the folly of criticising his college and his country by the lights of a false civilization. Hence as anyone can read, all Lukes structures on his college and his country are condemnatory of his own attitude. ... The book therefore discredits not Maynooth teaching, and certainly not scholastic teaching, but those who discredit such teaching from afar.

Luke Delmege went on to be a very successful book despite the criticisms here in Ireland.

Canon Sheehan referred again to these criticisms of *Luke Delmege* in correspondence he had with an English priest, Canon Wilfred Dallow of Upton, Birkinhead.

> *... I am so pleased that you like this book. ... I think you will read with interest the enclosed notices on a book that met with such a hostile reception at home. .....*

America gave a much more favourable reception to it as they invariably did to all his books. He once wrote "America must remain my happy hunting ground." The book was highly thought of also in Germany.

It wasn't all criticism of course here at home. Because of *My New Curate's* success Canon Sheehan was building up a great readership and his rising popularity was creating him into a celebrity, something that he didn't want as we see in a letter he wrote to Fr. Heuser in America.

> *Ir always gives me the shivers to see my name in print: and the little notoriety I have attained has been productive of annoyance rather than pleasure to me. I am dragged hither and thither by all sorts of demands; and as my health is always an uncertain quantity, I have to refuse all kinds of invitations to preach, lecture, etc.*

He was now the author of four books and before they had ever been written he had contributed to a series of papers in the Weekly Register under the general heading *"Books That Have Influenced Me."* In those contributions he said:

> I cannot now remember who was the kind friend that placed the books in my hands; but I cannot easily forget the sensation of wonder and surprise and delight when the music and the mystery of *"In Memoriam"* and the Promthean wisdom of Carlyle's *"Past and Present"* were revealed to me. It was far back in the sixties, and in halls where literature had to be studied sureptitiously. ... But if Tennyson influenced sentiment or created taste. Carlyle made a deeper, more profound and more lasting impression.

Some years later, however, a more mature Sheehan studying Carlyle could not accept his opinion of the Papacy and of the Catholic Church and wrote:

> I closed Carlyle for ever ... for the steady companion of my maturer years - Jean Paul. ... In professional studies my deepest attachment is to St. Augustine, whose 'City of God' though read fragmentarily had a profound influence on my mind.

Luke Delmege was published in book form by Messrs. Longmans, Green & Co. in 1901 and the year before saw the American publishers Marlier, Callanan & Co. bring out his book of poems *Cithara Mea*. The book, on the whole, had a religious theme running through it. Apart from a number of poems under the heading 'Miscellanea' and also some sonnets, the book's contents were basically divided into two subjects which Canon Sheehan called 'The Hidden' and 'The Revealed'. The former showed the poet looking as it were for the light of faith to understand the mysteries of life and the latter the reception of that light. The poems were very much the work of an intellectual, pensive, deep thinking, often sad with a sense of hopelessness as in the lines:

> We see the childlike helplessness of earth
> Its leaves and buds that grope in vain for Thee
> For Thee, the Father of an abandoned birth
> Wondering and weak for its own mystery.

Cithara Mea did not make any great impact, its contents being rather too intellectual. Nevertheless, it was appreciated by many friends of Fr. Sheehan. One such friend in England Dr. Barry said in a letter to him:

> On turning the leaves I catch a happy phrase or a fleeing thought and I seemed to understand you even better than from your stories.

Fr. Russell was very appreciative of the book even though he did not pretend to fully understand all that had been written and published. A number of the poems had appeared in the *Irish Monthly*.

Canon Sheehan was, by now, a very well established author. *My New Curate's* success being chiefly responsible. In a comprehensive discussion with an old friend he said:

> "I don't wonder you are surprised at the success of "My New Curate". Most people are - but none of them so astounded as myself. But I find my celebrity a little embarassing, if only on account of the enormous amount of correspondence it entails."

The conversation took place at his home in Doneraile around the time that the serialisation of *Luke Delmege* was drawing to a close in the *Ecclesiastical Review* and in answer to a question about it he said:

> "Yes "Luke Delmege" is nearly all printed but bringing it out in book form will involve a good deal of work, especially as I am not yet decided how far I may introduce changes into it. This also involves correspondence and moreover, I have at all times a good deal of parish work to attend to.

His friend referred to the large amount of letters the author got from total strangers and he replied:

> "Letters which one is loth to neglect. For instance I could show you numbers of letters from clergy of various denominations in England and America, thanking me for "My New Curate" as giving them an entirely new revelation as to

what a Catholic priest really is. They seem hardly to believe that we priests are made of flesh and blood. ... I do feel more than formerly a sense of responsibility which at times is almost burdensome. ... I cannot conceal from myself that there is a certain importance attaching to my writing if only from the fact (which is attested by the *Boston Pilot*) that I have now half-a-million readers in America alone. Again I hold a letter from a German Baron to say that the German translation of *"My New Curate"* has created quite a sensation in Germany.

When asked about his feeling of responsibility with regard to his writing, Fr. Sheehan remarked that he was not easily understood and therefore superficial readers were apt to misinterpret him. He felt that his words but half interpreted his thoughts and that his meaning was but faintly grasped. His conversationalist commented that he had now got the verdict of the world on his side and he replied:

"Yes, I hope I have the verdict of the educated and the intelligent. I have often preached to my people here that there is but one thing to fear - and that is ignorance. What I fear is that my writings may be read by the ignorant and perhaps perverted to evil purposes."

The conversation that took place was never intended initially to be published but the material was so interesting that the interviewer later wrote to him seeking permission to publish an account of the interview, which he readily gave. His friend remarked that he himself was well conversant with the book of poems *Cithara Mea* and added that he thought he detected the influence of Tennyson in the spirit, though not in the form of many poems, to which he replied:

"I may have been under his spell formerly but not now. If I had to acknowledge any master, it would be rather Shelly. I mean the Poet not the Atheist."

There was "hardly any true motif" for writing *My New Curate*, he told his friend. When asked if he agreed with the general verdict that it was his best book to date Fr. Sheehan said that by no means did he think so.

"The book I put my whole soul into was *The Triumph Of Failure* and naturally I care the most about it."

Referring to it and *Geoffrey Austin* Canon Sheehan said:

The two must be taken together as expressing a single idea. It is not fair to criticise them as stories. I never imagined that I had any one qualification for the novel writer who has a profession of his own and one different from mine. I merely used the story as a vehicle for expressing any views on religious subjects."

CHAPTER ELEVEN

Canon Sheehan's next literary contribution was a book he called *Under The Cedars And The Stars*, often judged to be one of his finest works. It appeared initially in America in *The Dolphin* magazine in 1902 in serial form. Now that his name was firmly established it was on every contribution.

Under The Cedars And The Stars was well received in America. There was no story as such, in fact it was a complete change of writing style for the author. It was a series of pen pictures set under four main headings Spring, Summer, Autumn and Winter. The sketches were personal and deep thinking, touching on practically all aspects of life and its meaning; nature and all its beauties and wonders: Poets and Philosophers and of course The Supernatural. Throughout the series he flitted from one theme to another. His Spring section opened with a description of his garden.

> My garden looks well just now, although the cold lingers, and
> now and again a shower of hail flung from some refrigator
> high up in the heavens threatens to break the fragile stems
> of my tulips and to scatter the white, milky blossoms on my
> apple trees.

From simple themes he switches to intellectual ones, to modern heresy and on to the Divinity of Christ. The author's descriptive powers really shine through in the series. There is Sheehan the Philosopher, the Poet, and the Man of God.

Under The Cedars And The Stars was brought out in book form in America by Benziger Brothers of New York and in 1903 Messrs Brown and Nolan published it for the Catholic Truth Society of Ireland. It was a rather thick volume and was priced at five shillings. There were, of course, the usual criticisms which eventually drew from Canon Sheehan the remark in a letter to Fr. Heuser in March 1903:

> What a wonderful literature we should have, if even one
> tenth of our critics would write something themselves.

Maurice Egan, an American who later became US Ambassador to Denmark took him to task for abandoning his writing of stories and indulging in literary and philosophical reflections. The Canon's Jesuit friend in Dublin Fr. Russell however continued to interject whenever the critics lash began to hurt and referring to *Under The Cedars And The Stars* wrote to him saying:

> Follow your own inspirations bravely to the end and make this perhaps the most beautiful of all your books. Critics will constantly refer to the standard of My New Curate - "Uneasy lies the head that wears a crown."

All in all, the reception of *Under the Cedars And The Stars* was favourable.

Following its publication in Ireland in 1903, the author, had a play published in 1904 by Messrs. Longmans, Green and Co. It was called *Lost Angel Of A Ruined Paradise.* It was not a success and the author was strongly advised to stick to what he was best at in the literary field. There were thirteen scenes in the drama representing the vocational attraction of young girls who had just left school. Canon Sheehan intended the drama to be presented by girls and the proceeds from both the presentation and the book were to benefit the Temple Street Hospital in Dublin for sick children.

Writing about his forray into drama, his friend Fr. Russell said with some candour:

> ... probably like Tennyson and his "Queen Mary", you prefer the *"Lost Angel of a Ruined Paradise"* to your stories. If so, you are greatly mistaken. ...

It was the Canon's first and only adventure into the field of drama. *The Irish Monthly* wasn't over enthusiastic about the publication and remarked that he was

> most at home, as he is bound to be, among the priests and people of Ireland; and none of them figure on the stage on which this "drama of modern life" is for the most part played.

Canon Sheehan's literary skills were now in full flight and a historical novel that he had been working on was accepted by Fr. Heuser for serialisation in *The Dolphin*. The story was *Glenanaar* and it ran from November 1904 to August 1905. Messrs Longmans Green and Co. published it in book form.

Glenanaar like *My New Curate* was an extremely popular book and one which found its way into many Irish homes. It was loosely based on a famous incident in 1829 called "*The Doneraile Conspiracy* ". Although that incident had happened three quarters of a century before the story was written, the sensitive nature of the subject which had as one of its ingredients that most hated of traits "the informer", it was the first time that anyone had dealt with the conspiracy through the medium of the novel. The central character in the book was Terence Casey, an Irish American, grandson of an informer named Daly. Casey's mother was the supposed child of the informer and abandoned by its parents. The child was taken in by a farmer named Edmond Connors, one of those accused by Daly in the conspiracy. And so there is the story of intrigue, but also of romance. Centre point of the novel is the actual trial for conspiracy and the famous ride of William Burke to Derrynane to get Daniel O'Connell come to Cork and defend those accused. In the real Doneraile Conspiracy trial of 1830, Edmond Connors was acquitted because of lack of evidence not because of anything Patrick Daly, the informer, said in his favour. Also Edmond Connors is portrayed in Canon Sheehan's book as coming from Glenanaar. He actually came from Buttervant parish. Terence Casey and his mother Nodhlag, the supposed child of the informer Daly, are purely fictional characters and had no bearing on the conspiracy.

In a letter dated 25th September 1904, Canon Sheehan wrote to Fr. Heuser:

> I *think' Glenanaar', though short, is the most perfect piece of work I have yet executed. I spelled the name of the romance phonetically - Glenanaar, as it is usually pronounced here. But perhaps I would spare myself some criticism from the Gaelic League if the word were printed correctly - Glenanair.*

On the whole, *Glenanaar* `was well received and Canon Sheehan's friend Fr. Russell kept him updated on reviews.

An article in the 1989 *Mallow Field Club Journal* by Mr. Con Power refers to *Glenanaar* and how Canon Sheehan got the idea of writing it. It was at a "Stations" breakfast in the Power home at Ballywalter, Shanballymore where the landlord George Bond Low was being discussed.

> The conversation turned to the Doneraile Conspiracy and Bond Low's involvement. Canon Sheehan, in his capacity as Parish priest of the district, was at the breakfast and it was suggested to him that he should write a book on "the Conspiracy". Subsequently, he visited Ballywalter many times for discussions with my father on the subject, patching together the story of those troubled times in and around Doneraile. The result was the novel we all loved so well - *Glenanaar*. At the next "Stations" in the house, the Canon said "It was here I got the idea - I hope you enjoyed the book."

To help him with his research the Canon had access to some old newspaper files in the home of a friend Philip Harold Barry, J. P. He also proceeded further and got permission to examine the court records of the trial.

In a reference to *Glenanaar,* the author M. P. Linehan in his book *Canon Sheehan of Doneraile* had this to say:

> The book came to be written this way. In the Canon's parish of his native town of Mallow there were many distinguished members of the old Munster legal circuit. One of them drew his attention to the materials for this romance that the records of the conspiracy provided. He prepared to act on the suggestion. A book had been published dealing with the circuit and giving details of the events leading up to the "Conspiracy" and the subsequent trial. It was unfortunately out of print but a diligent search was made throughout the neighbourhood for it. My father heard of the matter and having some old newspapers giving a record of the trial, he passed them on to the Canon.

In its review of the book in August 1905 the "New Ireland Review" was fullsome in its praise which it called a volume of romantic history in which all the characters are very real. No one, it said, but a close student of Irish village life could depict the social habits of the peasantry in so thoroughly natural a manner as Canon Sheehan. While the theme of *Glenanaar* was The Doneraile Conspiracy, the *New Ireland Review* also saw in the book a plea to wealthy Irish exiles in America to come back to the old country.

As Canon Sheehan's fame grew, he was in constant demand both as a lecturer and as a literary contributor to periodicals. There was much he had to refuse. Despite the criticism that he had suffered at the hands of some of the clergy, he was invited to address the Maynooth students in the *Aula Maxima* of the College on the 1st December 1903. The titles of his lecture was called *The Dawn of the Century*. Some of it was of a philosophical nature, eminently suited to his listeners.

> The great majority of you, gentlemen, are destined to spend your lives in the service of your own people, and in your native land. Happy are you beyond the apostles of your race abroad, for you will have the most faithful and deeply-religious people on earth to minister to - a people who will look up to you with a kind of idolatory as the representative of all they revere in time and eternity. ... the Irish priest must be in advance of his people, educationally, by at least fifty years. The priests have the lead and they must keep it.
> ...

It was in 1905 that Canon Sheehan's book *A Spoiled Priest* and *Other Stories* came out and in the following year Messrs Longman published in book form his *Early Essays and Lectures*.

The Canon had considerable understanding of the land problems in Ireland and of their social implications. For some time he had been putting together a story that dealt with the subject and about the evils of landlordism. He called the story *Lisheen*. Again, like many of his previous works, it was first serialised in America. The "Catholic World" of New York carried it and it was then published in book form in 1907.

The story is centered around an idealistic landlord named Maxwell who decides to live the life of a peasant, a farming family named McAuliffe, a retired army officer named Outram and also a landlord

101

and Englishman named Hammerton. Caught in the midst of them all is Fr. Cosgrove. It was an attempt on Sheehan's part to show how perhaps the land problem might be solved and so redress the enormous flight from the land.

In a letter that Canon Sheehan received from a friend asking why he wrote *Lisheen* he replied to his correspondent in verse as follows:

> Why did I write Lisheen? ... To show
> The claims of brotherhood and kin;
> The deep broad streams of Love that flow
> In peers' and peasants' hearts - the sin
> Of broken blighted vows - the Fate
> That follows over land and sea
> On wheel and rudder, them that flee
> The boundless bounds of the estate
> Of Right and Law inviolate!
> If Nemesis relentless be
> And Fate has seals of certainty
> The spirit that has borne the test
> Of spirits ranks among the best -
> The bravest who aspires to be
> The bayward of Humanity.

While *Lisheen* didn't in any way create the impression that *My New Curate* or *Glenanaar* did, nevertheless it was a worthwhile exercise for its author. It highlighted the evils of landlordism and showed also how vast improvements in the land question could be achieved.

Again there were those who saw in the book "more of the sameness" such as the critic in the *Dublin Review* who wrote:

> Perhaps Canon Sheehan does not think his public capable of entering into more difficult economic questions and we are the more led to think this, as we have long been of opinion that he has too great a contempt for his readers. He cannot believe that we are really contented with anything so simple and so homely as the Irish poor.

Canon Sheehan's great American friend and correspondent Justice Oliver Wendell Holmes liked *Lisheen* but saw flaws in characterisation. He wrote:

> *I think your fashionable people and men of the world are not quite so real as your peasants; and I wonder whether there is not implied too wholesome a condemnation of the fashionable world.*

It was a shrewd observation and one that had already been made. Canon Sheehan took little time to study the characters of those already referred to and so they often came across in his writings as unreal in contrast to the rural characters which he portrayed very accurately.

His next book was initially called 'The Blindness of the Very Rev. Dr. Gray". He also had another title for it "The Final Law". Fr. Heuser, was on a visit to him in Doneraile at that time when the Canon was beginning to feel the first effects of an illness that would eventually destroy him physically. Recording the visit later Fr. Heuser said:

> Time sped amid these interesting sidelights of the Canon's activities. But I had come to obtain, if possible, fresh material for the *Ecclesiastical Review*. When I broached the subject he alertly arose, and, reaching to his desk, took out a packet of manuscript, the kind with which I had become familiar through the past years.
>
> "Here" he said "is what I have been working on for some time. It will probably be the last thing I shall be able to do. For I feel my time on earth is measured; and I am a bit weary."

It wasn't to be by any means the last. There were, as we shall see, a number of books yet to come. The manuscript he showed Fr. Heuser later became *The Blindness Of Dr. Gray*. The story wasn't completely filled in although the last chapter was. At any rate when Canon Sheehan made the necessary adjustments to the manuscript, it was published in serial form in the *American Ecclesiastical Review*, the first instalment appearing in November 1907. The entire serialisation spanned almost two years. It was brought out in book form towards the end of 1909 by Messrs Longman Green & Co. of London.

The Blindness of Dr. Gray was the last of Canon Sheehan's clerical novels. It had a mixed reception, comparisons invariably being made with *My New Curate* and its great character Daddy Dan. Nevertheless, it became a popular enough book with Irish readers. The story was set around a parish priest and his curate, the former Dr. Gray being the very anthitisis of that lovable priest in *My New Curate*. Dr. Gray saw everything in black and white with no room for shading in between. Human frailities are not understood or tolerated. The people whom he serves obey and respect him to a certain degree. He is not loved by them and neither do they trust him. He is now old with failing sight and his orphaned niece from America, who is a nurse and who has lived with him for some years decides to accompany an ill boy abroad to help him recover. There is consternation and her stern guardian lashes out.

> I have to consider the interests of my flock which, at least as yet, has not abandoned the old Christian ideas of maiden modesty and prudence. Hence I gave my niece the alternative of staying at home with me or leaving me forever. She took her choice. And I have cut her image out of my heart forever.

It was said that the character Dr. Gray was based on a Cloyne Priest of earlier times - Canon "Danger' Murphy. The author did not agree. However, there were certainly traits and idiosyncrasies indicative of him and probably of many other priests taken to mould this stern character.

The Blindness Of Dr. Gray was a fine story and very much addressed to the Irish Clergy. Dr. Gray was highlighted for us in some respect by Canon Sheehan's description of Canon Murphy in his essay *'Moonlight of Memory.'* William O'Brien wrote of the same man:

> My earliest religious relations were with a singular and stern-looking priest, over six feet in height, a scholar, a solitary man, whose face was seldom softened with a smile and who came to be known to the awe-stricken parishioners as 'Canon Danger'. His eyes would diffuse a band of

'mitching' schoolboys, or clear the Navigation Road of whispering lovers as effectively as a troop of dragoons.

In a Book Notice which appeared in the *Irish Ecclesiastical Record* early in 1910 there was this to say about *The Blindness Of Dr. Gray.*

> But to come to Dr. Gray, we confess we found the old gentleman rather gloomy and depressing, that we thought his curate rather priggish and pedantic and that his niece appeared to us anything but convincing in her relations with the Wycherleys. ... Apart from the general drawbacks there is the usual fine writing, with gleams of sly humour and deep insight into certain phases of human nature.

In 1908 Canon Sheehan had produced a companion volume to *Under The Cedars And The Stars* called *Parerga*. Both formats were identical. Many aspects of life were touched upon and there were some fine pen potraits as in his recollections of an Irish sea-side holiday. The location was Ballycotton, Co. Cork.

> And I have pleasant memories too of a short holiday which I took this Summer. I had not been to this seaside village for thirty five years - since my student days; but I carried always with me the recollection of its one street, wind-swept and sloping down to the sea, a naked island; and just beyond, the white walls of the lighthouse. ... And there was one sheltered spot, where the flat face of a rock fronted the sea and formed a kind of natural seat or lounge where in my adolescence I read, and read and read the livelong day.

Early in 1911 another book from the Canon's pen appeared called *The Intellectuals* with a sub-title "An Experiment in Irish Club-Life." It was again published by Longmans Green & Co. It was a departure both in style and theme from his usual works. Among the several characters were an Irishman, an Englishman, and a Scotsman. In the mix of races was a Protestant and a Catholic and the group was also made up from different social strata. They were all Club members. It was an attempt by the author to show that people of differing social, cultural and religious backgrounds could live together as one nation. In the book's preface he said that his object in writing it was "to show that there are really no invincible antagonisms amongst the peoples who make up the commonwealth of Ireland, no mutual repugnances that may not be removed by a freer and kindlier intercourse with each other."

William O'Brien had much in praise for the book and its author. In a letter dated 11th March 1911 to the Canon he made some interesting observations.

> Nearly everything you depict as to the friendly mingling of races and creeds would be possible if you could only realise your first postulate - viz that a tolerant and sympathetic-minded Irish priest should be the inspiring force of the reunion. Alas and Alas! that postulate is the one hardest to supply. The bishops and priests in general, in place of playing that glorious part are (unconsciously of course) the principal force in making the enemies of peace and National Regeneration supreme.

In its June issue of 1911, the *Irish Review* was anything but complimentary in its comments on *The Intellectuals*.

> ... What is one to say of such a book? As a work of fiction, it is frankly wearisome. ... As a picture of the society dealt with, it may be valuable, though extremely depressing. ... Canon Sheehan's aspirations for the breaking down of sectarian and race barriers are obviously sincere.

The Intellectuals was not a popular book. However everything Canon Sheehan wrote was always contrasted with *My New Curate* and much of his work suffered because of that.

It was in the year 1911 also that his book *The Queen's Fillet* was published. The story was set in the days of the French Revolution. The author wrote the book to show the great excesses that were perpetrated through revolution often with a total disregard for human life. He saw perhaps what could happen and did in fact happen in his own country. In his book he said:

> The Royalists have studied under the Revolution; and it will go hard if the pupils do not outstrip their masters in barbarity.

106

How right he was as evidenced in Ireland with the savage atrocities of Civil War.

Maurice Francis Egan of the American Legation in Copenhagen in a letter to the Canon dated August 12th 1911 thanking him for a copy of the book had this to say about it:

> *You seem to have absorbed the sentiments of the time, controlled them, combined them and presented them to us with a force that has not been equaled. ... I do not think that the love element is sufficiently accentuated and the wife of the hero is really only a shadow. ... It is a solid book but I find that having created "My New Curate" you sometimes suffer by comparison with your only rival - yourself. I wish you had put more of the human feeling which glows in "My New Curate" into this admirable picture.*

In a letter to Fr. Russell dated 29th August 1911 Canon Sheehan commented on his latest publication.

> *Many thanks for special copy of the I. Monthly, for your own gracious critique and for the extracts of notices from the reviewer. They have all been singularly, I might say, surprisingly favourable; and the Americans are even more generous than the English. In a fortnight after publication, 1500 copies of the six-shilling Edition and 1100 copies of the Colonial edition had been sold, so everything looks well for the book. ... I think I have been fully impartial all round. I have not spared the noblesse nor the Jacobin, nor the Bourbon in trying to exemplify my two favourite theories:*
>
> (a) *That injustice begets injustice.*
> (b) *That fear has been the cause of the world's greatest crimes.*

The harshness of criticism by the Catholic Press towards Canon Sheehan's books was referred to by himself in a letter to Fr. M. J. Phelan S.J. on January 8th 1913.

> *... Let me say at once then, that I feel deeply indebted to you for such kind words about myself and my books. They are all*

the more valuable as coming from your pen on the principle that it is the highest distinction: Laudari a Laudato.

And also because such an expression of opinion is rather a rare experience of mine; for the whole, I have not received much favour from the Catholic Press. The very book (The Queen's Fillet) which you appreciate so highly, received but scant, and decidedly unfavourable notice from two such Catholic Journals as the "Month" and the "Catholic World". This is all the more strange, because the entire secular Press of the world wrote kindly of the book but it is useless to dwell on these things, except to emphasise one's appreciation of a Catholic Critic like yourself. ...

In fact, as far back as March 1899, Canon Sheehan in a letter to Fr. Heuser had this to say regarding the Catholic Press when referring to a well known Catholic priest writing in England:

... Fancy, he never received a line of encouragement during all the years he was writing for Catholic Reviews. He is supporting his church and mission by his pen. ... For the years I was writing for the Irish Ecclesiastical Record I never received one word of encouragement. You and my dear friend Fr. Russell are the only priests that have ever said a kindly word of my work hitherto. ...

Canon Sheehan was still working on two books, *Miriam Lucas* and *The Graves at Kilmorna*. The former was the last of his books that he was to see published.

Miriam Lucas published by Longmans Green & Co was a story divided into three where the reader was taken from the shores of Cork Harbour and the East Ferry area to Dublin and Trinity College, from there to New York and back again to Ireland. "Glendarragh" the fictional great house above East Ferry where the lovely Miriam Lucas lives plays a prominent part in the Canon Sheehan story because of the curse on it whereby no heir will be born there. There were some fine pen pictures of many of the characters, not least that of the rector the Rev. Crosthwaite. It was a fine story, a study of Irish society complicated by religious prejudice and class. Some of the characters were perhaps painted larger than life but always with sympathy. By and large the book was well received but as with most of Canon Sheehan's books, it had its critics. Summing up the book, the *"Irish Ecclesiastical Record"* had this to say in February 1913:

> In attacking the complex social problems of life in Ireland at the present day he (the author) over-estimates the factors and rather gives us an idea of the state of things which might exist did particular phases become general and types dominant. ... while the background is too heavy and elaborate, and the description too detailed, the author has made everything contribute to working out the fate of *Miriam Lucas* to a happy issue.

In Canon Sheehan's literary life there was one episode towards its end which proved to be a tragic one for students of his work. It was the destruction of his Memoirs. His early biographer tells us that among the manuscripts he had completed were two volumes of his memoirs. "These" the Canon said "will not be published until after my death." He gave Fr. Heuser the impression that they contained reflections upon his own work, the difficulties and disappointments that he had encountered and the mistakes made by himself as well as by his critics. Referring to those memoirs in a letter to Fr. Russell dated 8th December 1911 he said:

> *They are not intended for print at anytime. I wrote them about eight years ago just to preserve them for my own amusement. There is another Fasciculus dealing with my life in Doneraile as an author: but it is not complete.*

Towards the end of 1911 Canon Sheehan completed another novel which he said he was "holding in reserve". It was not published before he died in 1913 and in fact did not appear until the Spring of 1915. It too was published by Messrs Longman Green & Co. The book was called *The Graves At Kilmorna* and dealt with the rise and fall of Fenianism. It drew some of its inspiration from the Mallow area. Below Sheehan's residence in the town was the glen where the local men of 1867 drilled. Carmichael's Lane was ythe hiding place for the rifles etc. beyond the market place and "the grey old Geraldine keep beside the Castle where the local English magnate, old Sir Denham Norreys lived and ruled, looked up from among the trees beyond Gallows Hill Lane."

Much of the author's recollections as a student such as the death of Peter O'Neill Crowley and the Mallow election of 1865 permeate the story. Also the author's time on the English Mission following his ordination is reflected in the young priest who set out to Dartmoor from Exeter to bring religious solace to the Catholic convicts. The main part of the story is historical fact but the book ends up without hope, a tragic end where violence plays no mean part. Because of its Fenian association the book had considerable Irish appeal but it also had some severe critics, among them being the novelist Katherine Tynan, herself the author of over 50 books. She had this to say:

> From the literary point of view I lay down *The Graves at Kilmorna* with a conviction that as literature it is nothing. That it is crammed full with gentleness and idealism and high-mindedness is quite another matter. These qualities make Canon Sheehan a teacher, a preacher, a voice crying in the wilderness, but they do not make him a literary man. ...
> As a story, *The Graves at Kilmorna* is nothing: as a revelation of disillusionment and bitterness in a noble soul with a world, which perhaps had to be broken before being re-made, it is much.

Were Canon Sheehan alive to read such a critique, he would no doubt be hurt but it had come from the pen of a very eminent writer. In an early draft of the biography of Canon Sheehan that Fr. Heuser had been working on, he sent parts of it to Denis B. Sheehan, brother of the late Canon for his comments. He was pleased at what he had read despite the fact that much of the Canon's correspondence etc. had not yet come into Heuser's possession but was not at all pleased at the observations made on *The Graves of Kilmorna* and in a letter dated 23rd September 1916 Mr. Sheehan had this to say:

> *I was somewhat disappointed at your slight reference to the "Graves at Kilmorna" in the biography, especially as this book is considered in many ways as the most powerful of his books.*
> *Mr. Blackwood (Blackwood and Sons, Publishers) told me that it was the finest and most thrilling book of the day and I send you a bundle of newspaper cuttings (thro Messrs Longman) which show how it has appealed to all sections of the Press in every country.*

> It is considered the truest picture of the national soul of Ireland and has been welcomed as the strongest appeal to national feeling and sentiment ever made to our people.
>
> In view of recent events it is almost prophetic and I hope you will give larger space to this book and dwell on its true and deep illumination of the strong deepseated feeling of Nationality in Ireland..

Fr. Heuser took note of what the late Canon's brother had written and dealt with the book more extensively than he otherwise would have done.

Among Canon Sheehan's papers was an unfinished and unedited manuscript of a novel which he had called *Tristram Lloyd*. The incomplete story tells us perhaps that the author may not have thought it was worth finishing or that he was unable to give it the end which he would have liked. The manuscript was completed by Rev. Henry Gaffney, O.P. He carried out an extremely difficult task very ably and competently and the book was brought out in 1929 by the Talbot Press of Dublin. It did not create any stir whatever.

Fr. Heuser who was responsible for the serialisation of most of Canon Sheehan's work and who was probably one of his closest literary confidants was happy with the finished work, feeling that it would have been a pity if it hadn't been completed and he wrote a biographical introduction to the book.

> ... The Editor has been extremely reluctant to interfere with the Canon's manuscript or with his trend of thought. Therefore, there are in the novel of necessity, many things which invite criticism if the untimely death of Canon Sheehan and the Editor's intention be not in the critic's perspective.
>
> A literary fragment of this nature must either be relegated to oblivion or published under judicious editorship. The Publishers have chosen the latter alternative, confident that their decision will be applauded by all lovers of the gentle Canon of Doneraile. They know that those who have caught the Canon's apostolic message in his other writings will not miss it in the story of Tristram Lloyd.

All in all, Canon Sheehan's literary output was phenomenal. Although he had done the groundwork for some of his earlier works before he came to Doneraile as parish priest, nevertheless it was while pastor there from 1895 to his death in 1913 that he produced the following:

Geoffrey Austin, Student; The Triumph Of Failure; My New Curate; Luke Delmege: The Blindness of Dr. Gray; Glenanaar; Lisheen; Miriam Lucas; The Graves at Kilmorna; The Queen's Fillet; A Spoiled Priest and Other Stories. Also from his pen came Early Essays and Lectures; Under the Cedars and the Stars; Parerga; The Intellectuals; Cithara Mea (Poems); Lost Angel of a Ruined Paradise (Drama); Mariae Corona (Sermons).

Added to these there were the numerous essays, literary criticisms, lectures etc. It wa a fantastic achievement from a man very devoted to his parish and whose health was always suspect.

CHAPTER TWELVE

As mentioned earlier, Canon Sheehan embarked on a correspondence and friendship with the American Jurist Justice Oliver Wendell Holmes Jnr. in the Autumn of 1903 following an introduction by Lord and Lady Castletown of Doneraile Court. Holmes had been on one of his visits to them and the Castletowns, as was customary, had the Canon to meet any of their guests which they felt he would be interested in. Except for meeting on a couple of occasions over the following ten years, their contact was through letters, each letter drawing the two men closer to each other, each contact gaining more respect, tolerance and understanding for the other's point of view and for each other's beliefs.

In many ways, it was the most intriguing of friendships between opposites - Sheehan the priest, profound believer in God and in man's destiny, Holmes on the other hand very much the non believer, with the brilliant mind. Yet they became the closest of friends. It is interesting to see from their letters their views on life, on literature and on the great philosophers. Their lives were in sharp contrast. Canon Sheehan, without doubt one of the best read men of his day in Ireland derived much from his books and from his vocation as a priest. He missed out, however, on social contacts with great and open minds. Holmes on the other hand had a much more liberal education, with a view on the meaning of life that Sheehan couldn't accept, yet he also was a great man, a man of honour, of integrity and of compassion. Today he is widely regarded as the nearest thing to a great philosopher that America has yet produced. He was born in 1841 and served 50 years on the Supreme Court of Massachusetts and the United States.

Oliver Wendell Holmes had been wounded three times while serving as an officer in the American Civil War and went on to become a very distinguished lawyer, fully recognised as such in many parts of the world. He was a Professor of Law at Harvard, associate Justice and later Chief Justice of the Massachusets Judicial Supreme Court and Associate Justice of the Supreme Court of the United States. It is not easy to understand how two men of such differing beckgrounds became such intimate friends, each very much the guardian of his own philosophy. Yet their correspondence shows an intimacy and understanding that only friends could have.

Holmes truly admired the novelist priest from an Irish rural parish who was razor sharp in his observations of his fellow man and who was able to penetrate his own unbelieving mind. Holmes was also conscious of the fact that this very lucid minded priest saw him (Holmes) for what he was a "regular Danton-Herod on paper and in theory" but "not very hard hearted in practice."

The surviving correspondence over a ten year period 1903-1913 has gaps, with no letters at all covering the period November 1904 to August 1907. There is no doubt but that some letters were exchanged over this period, however their absence do not detract from the correspondence as a whole. In the case of Canon Sheehan, Holmes letters to him during that period may well have been destroyed if they were of a very controversial nature, as some months before his death the Canon wrote to Holmes and said that his (Holmes) letters had been "carefully filed and kept to be disposed of at your pleasure when I have gone."

Strangely enough, the correspondence surviving from Holmes to Sheehan are only transcripts. The original letters appeared to have been disposed of but not before Sheehan's biographer Fr. Heuser made copies of them. Following Sheehan's letter to Holmes in June 1913 telling him that his letters had been kept to be disposed of at his (Holmes) pleasure when the Canon had died, it is concievable that Holmes on learning of his friend's death asked that the letters be destroyed. This is borne out by the fact that when Fr. Heuser consulted Oliver Wendell Holmes about the correspondence when the former was working on the biography of Sheehan, Holmes wrote to Heuser saying:

I am disturbed to learn of the existence of my letters. I sometimes wrote confidentially and always with the freedom one practices to an intimate expecting no other eye to see them.

The correspondence between Holmes and Sheehan was of a very free flowing nature each telling the other what they thought or had done. It was sometimes on a very light vein, at other times serious and lengthy as when there was a clash of intellects and beliefs. But it was never laced with any acrimony even though each man was taking a stand.

It probably would be true to say that because of Canon Sheehan's great lack of intellectual discussion or debate in Doneraile, the letters from Holmes were a tonic for his lively mind. We learn little however about Doneraile and its people from the letters although they do show that Canon Sheehan's lack of visitors of an intellectual nature was a facet of his life that he found unfulfilled. The Castletowns, as already mentioned, introduced him to any people of learning who were their guests and on the occasions that Justice Holmes came from America and was a guest at Doneraile Court, he visited the Canon regularly as we glean from a letter dated 5th October 1907 to the Judge from the Canon.

> I sincerely hope that this has been by no means your final visit to us; but that you will find time during your long vacations to run over again and give us the great pleasure of seeing you. For your little morning visits to me were gleams of sunshine across a grey monotonous life; and I look back to them with pleasure, but also with the regret that such experiences should be so transient. I think I mentioned to you that I felt my greatest want to be some intercourse with minds whose ideas would act as a stimulant to thought, by casting new lights on old subjects. And although we agreed to differ on many points, it was very refreshing to me to be brought face to face with original thinking on the subjects that are of deepest interest to myself.

Agreeing to differ and mutual respect were the two ingredients that laid a solid foundation for their deep friendship and these things came into play early on in their association. Canon Sheehan sent presents of his books to Holmes as and when they were published. Towards the end of 1903 he had sent him *Under The Cedars And The Stars*. Acknowledging it, Holmes told him that he was greatly and unaffectedly charmed and moved by it. He did not or would not accept the validity of everything the author had written especially from a religious point of view and told him so:

> I am as far as possible from being on your side - but I still hope you will have room for a little pleasure when I say that your book moves me more intimately by old world feeling than anything that I have read for a great while and that if you did not regard me as an enemy I think it might be that we should recognise each other as friends. ... It is true that I don't

believe your philosophy - or shall I say, the religion you so beautifully exalt. ... But I love an idealist - even while I doubt the cosmic significance of your judgements.

The correspondence between the two men shows a side of Sheehan in tolerance and understanding that he did not show when commenting in his essays on many of the great English writers especially when they propounded their religious disbeliefs. Perhaps if he had had the opportunity to meet these people as he had done Holmes, he might have understood them more fully.

With Holmes he was able to be entirely open and frank:

We differ in our intrepretation of human life and the universe around us; but that fact, so far as I am concerned, in no way diminishes my esteem for you. I respect your conscientious convictions; nor have I any right to intrude within the sacred sanctuary, where each soul is alone with God. Conscience is the supreme monitor. I would that all men believe as I do, for I believe that this faith is not only the solution of what is otherwise inexplicable, but also the great proof and support of the human soul under the serious difficulties of life. But I have no right to force this conviction on you; and the fact, that you see with other eyes than mine, should in no way imperil or diminish the friendship, which I take the privilege of assuming, should subsist between us.

Over a ten year period the correspondence covered everything from Plato to Tennyson, from Holmes in his country house at Beverly Farms, Mass. to the Presbytery in Doneraile, from early Spring days in America to the golden days of Autumn along the Awbeg river. Although Holmes lived for ninety four years (1841-1935), he was concerned in March 1908 regarding age.

A week ago Sunday I passed a birthday. I am 67. I try to realise that the prospect is short.

The Canon eagerly looked forward to hearing from his friend.

Yours is one out of two or three handwritings, which when I recognise on an envelope, gives me a thrill of pleasure and compels me to leave my breakfast cool until I read it. The vast bulk of my correspondence I put aside until I have leisure; and some letters I should like to have the privilege of never opening.

The correspondence indicates a growing and deepening bond of friendship highlighted and accentuated from time to time by descriptive passages such as in the letter the Canon wrote from the Bay View Hotel in Ballycotton, Co. Cork on the 13th June 1909.

I am here for a quiet holiday above the eternal sea - that same sea that washes the shores beneath your delightful villa. It needs no violent stretch of the imagination to picture us shaking hands across that little span of waters. ... This is an antique out of this world, keltic and fishy village, just enlivened by the presence of a half dozen Londoners, who came over here from the smoke and fog and Babylon, to inhale some sweet air, and to exercise man's great privilege of destruction by killing all the fish they can, out upon the deep seas. It is not for food they kill but for "sport" to be able to say in a London club: "I killed a skate, weighing 125 pounds and several hundred conger eels".

Canon Sheehan was delighted to be able to tell Judge Holmes at the end of August 1909 that he had been offered a Bishopric but turned it down. His friend was delighted or as he once described himself 'your herectic friend.' The time was now approaching where the Canon could see the end of life's road coming into view.

The infirmities of age are creeping down on myself and I am becoming more home-tied every day, working on and trying to get in as much useful travail as I can before night falls.

He was only fifty eight years old when he wrote those words to Holmes but the terminal illness that was to take its toll in a few years was beginning to be felt. We gather too from the correspondence around that time that their mutual friends, Lord and Lady Castletown had run into some serious financial difficulties. Holmes asked his friend for some news of them in a letter he wrote from the Supreme Court in Washington on the 1st March 1911.

*Do you know anything about the Castletowns? I know they
have had reverses and I gather that he has collapsed, but I
can't ask Lady Castletown questions.*

The Canon was able to tell him that the Castletowns were actually in
financial trouble at that time. It happened apparently shortly after
they had returned from London where Lady Castletown had undergone
an eye operation. It would appear that the Castletowns were oblivious
to their financial problems. Referring to the situation in his letter of
reply to Holmes, Canon Sheehan went on to say:

*He (Lord Castletown) had sold out all the purchased estates;
and had speculated widly (so it was said) in foreign
investments, which proved useless. Receivers were at once
sent down here to take charge of everything. Lord C. is at
Granston; Lady C. in London. I understand they are allowed
£2000 each per annum; and the latest news is, that the estate
was not so involved as was at first supposed; and that
possibly they may be able to return at no very distant date.
Meanwhile, Sir John Arnott, who has rented the place for the
last few years during the hunting months has now taken over
the Court for 12 months. One of the sad things connected with
the affair was the destruction of the entire head of deer in
the Park.*

Canon Sheehan at this time was entering his sixieth year and, as he
told Justice Holmes, had no long lease on life. In fact in a letter to him
from his hospital bed in the South Infirmary in Cork on the 6th
October 1912 he said:

*I went on working until a sudden collapse came in June which
brought me to the gates of death. To my intense disgust and
regret, the doctors pulled me back from the "eternal rest" to
face the world as a chronic invalid. I have hopes of leaving
here and perhaps of resuming some parochial work; but life
for me is henceforth to be carried on a broken wing.*

Despite his grave illness the Canon carried on his correspondence with
Holmes who wrote him on many topics outside of illness "only because I
may amuse or distract you." Holmes was very distressed that his dear
friend was now so ill but the letters still crossed the Atlantic from his

sick bed and all were replied to. A ray of hope shone for the Canon when he got a short letter from him from Westminster telling him that he would come *"after the season here has ended."* Canon Sheehan replied the following day calling his letter *"a delightful piece of news"* and was pleased for the Castletowns whom he felt could do with a visitor. There appears to be no record as to whether the proposed visit came about or not.

This was the last letter of the Holmes-Sheehan correspondence. Space does not permit an in-depth assessment that such correspondence warrants but it reveals much about Canon Sheehan which otherwise would have gone unknown.

CHAPTER THIRTEEN

Canon Sheehan was a man of many parts, each of which he filled with distinction. He was first and foremost a priest, a spiritual leader of his people who, despite all the fame that his writing brought him, allowed it never to interfere in any way with the performance of his priestly duties.

It is worth looking briefly at the Roman Catholic Church in Ireland in the second half of the nineteenth century, a period into which Canon Sheehan had been born and in which he grew up and was ordained priest. In the 1840's there had been a considerable amount of friction among the Irish Hierarchy on political matters and also regarding National School education.

Rome was keeping a close eye on developments and decided to appoint a man who had been the Rector of the Irish College in Rome for about 20 years as Archbishop of Armagh and Primate of All-Ireland. He was Paul Cullen who had been very importantly placed as a close liason man between the Roman Curia and the Irish Bishops. An ardent supporter of ultramontanism or complete Papal authority, he set out to regulate as far as he was able the political behaviour of the Irish clergy. With regard to education, he opposed the Government's National Schools policy as he did the new Queen's Colleges in Belfast, Galway and Cork and endeavoured to establish his own Catholic University in Dublin.

Archbishop Cullen was appointed Archbishop of Dublin in 1852 and became the first Irish Cardinal. He played a major role with regard to the declaration of Papal Infallability at the first Vatican Council of 1870.

There were of course many Irish clergy who didn't see eye to eye with him in regard to their involvement in issues affecting their parishioners such as the Land League. It is interesting too to see how for example the practice of having the "Stations" in houses and of which Canon Sheehan was very much a part in Doneraile and referred to them in his writings, were frowned upon by Cardinal Cullen. The Council of Trent had laid down that the religious practices in Catholic

Europe be tied to the parish church and excluded any participation by household gatherings such as the "Stations" in Ireland.

At the Synod of Thurles in 1850 at which Cardinal Cullen was Papal Legate. "House Stations" had been forbidden. Many Irish bishops however, especially those in the Archdioceses of Cashel were not inclined to suppress the Station Masses as they still served a useful purpose in the practice of the Faith by the people. Cardinal Cullen made a determined effort to get Rome to condemn once and for all the practice. In this he was not successful and Rome finally allowed a limited toleration of the celebration of the "Station Masses" in private houses.

Canon Sheehan both as student and young priest must certainly have absorbed some of the ultramontanism promoted by Cardinal Cullen and also of course by many Bishops.

His background was middle class. He was however a very humble man and as mentioned earlier he was a great favourite with children. One who knew him recalled:

> He could never resist speaking to the children he met along the roads on his evening walks. He knew each by name and it was his delight to bend above them, patting their tossed hair and asking them questions.

His rather austere bearing was in sharp contrast to the priest who was the kindliest of men. A brilliant scholar, not greatly reflected in his time as a student in Maynooth, he would have been very much top of his league in the diocese of Cloyne. This coupled with the fact that his Bishop Dr. McCarthy had been his guardian while PP in Mallow following the death of his parents placed him well in the "pecking order" when promotions were being made. In fact he jumped the queue by twenty six places when he was appointed parish priest of Doneraile in 1895 at the rather young age of forty three. That promotion must have caused some murmurings among the clergy who were high up in the promotion list. Nevertheless, he was an extremely able man and through his great work as parish priest in Doneraile, the ailing parish was restored to full health after some years.

He had a great interest in education and the schools under his care came in for special attention. As well as the Presentation Convent and Christian Brothers school in Doneraile, there was a boys and a girls school in Shanballymore and three mixed schools as Skehana, Ballyvonare and Ballydaniel. He also provided entertainment for the young through drama, music and literature. His good friend Lady Castletown had a parish hall built in 1910 costing £400 at a time in fact when the Castletowns were experiencing financial problems themselves. The hall was a boon to the parish as it had a stage and various rooms for reading, billiards etc. Over the entrance to the hall was the inscription:

This Hall was erected by Lady Castletown in memory of her mother the Viscountess Doneraile, 1910.

The Viscountess was in fact a grand niece of Robert Emmet.

Among his many theories on education, Canon Shehan held the view that a boy or girl should be educated only to his or her station in life and then placed in employment. This would have been the middle class thinking of the time and he went on to say:

We hear a great deal about the "poor man's son" and the necessity of giving clever boys a chance of developing undoubted talents in the halls of some university. It is a spacious cry because it holds an element of truth - that it is a deordination in nature to have splendid talents allowed to run to waste; and to see brave young geniuses who might be Newtons or Lavaters condemned for life to the spade and matlock.

Such a view would have been the view of many Catholic clergy in Ireland at the time because of the fear of the rise of socialism. To have the poor man's son educated to a high degree could mean that the authority of the clergy may be weakened or challenged. Nevertheless much of what the Canon advocated in the fields of Primary, Secondary and University education were the result of very deep study and while in the modern Ireland of today, much of his thinking would be looked upon as old fashioned, his theories were of a very practical nature for the early part of this century.

Canon Sheehan got on extremely well with other denominations and was thought very highly by them. A shy man, he was aptly described by a friend who called to see him when he was curate in Mallow for the second time

..... to the quiet house shut away from the public highway by a grove of tall trees. There in the ways, set apart for the curate and his reverend pastor we see the future Canon walking slowly in the shade or seated on the cutaway stump of a tree with the foliage of the side growth all around him. I once came upon him there reading leisurely ... books were his principal friends; his personal associates were few and while to all he was the devoted, considerate consoling priest, ever kind in adversities and ever helpful in perplexities, his paths always led to the secluded ways on which the light of celebrity never shone.

He fulfilled his sacred ministry with dignity, integrity and compassion. Recollections of him as a priest were related long after he had passed away, all without exception being high in praise of a saintly man.

His early biographer, Fr. Heuser writing a few years after his death said:

No one who met the pastor of Doneraile casually would from his appearance suspect that he was the man who introduced the genial, whole-hearted Irish parish priest "Daddy Dan" in *My New Curate* to the literary world. ...But when the Canon received a visitor in the presbytery, the distant and courtly dignity of his manner took on the priestly glow of cordiality. ... and his wide range of information would reveal a wholly different man from what the outer shell suggested. ... There was a remarkable air of order and English tidiness about everything in and around the house. No token of luxury or self-indulgence; on the contrary, a certain severity everywhere excepting perhaps in the dining room. ... The upper room, fitted up as a library, contained only a meagre selection of volumes. But they were choice in quality - English, French, German, Italian. ...

I belong to the Thomas Davis School of Politics which would band all Irishmen in one common phalanx for the betterment of our common country.

wrote Canon Sheehan to a friend. Following the passing of the Land Acts he saw a type of nationalism developing which could mean replacing one ascendancy with another. He highlighted this in articles he wrote in the early days of the Cork Free Press. He in fact wrote the main editorial in that paper's first issue.

Having pointed out the great wrongs that Ireland suffered and were still suffering under an alien government, his idea of Conference and Conciliation to force change was always an underlying theme. He saw the changes that were coming about in Ireland and referring to democracy he posed the question:

But who are the people and who are embraced under the word that bears such momentous significance - the democracy of Ireland? Certainly, it does not mean a section of the people. The very word excludes such a meaning. Certainly it does not mean predominance of any one class or form of religious belief.

Canon Sheehan supported Home Rule. He resented, however, the comments of men like Sir Horace Plunkett who intimated that much of the blame for Ireland's backward state was the fault of the Irish clergy through what he regarded as extravagent church building instead of promoting industrial activity in the country. Plunkett was the founder of the Co-operative movement in Ireland and in fact one of the first two of his co-operative establishments was set up in Doneraile's main street in 1899 following discussions he had with Lord Castletown and two local men Robert Andrew Anderson and Alexis Roche.

Plunkett's contribution to improve the lot of Irish farming was indeed very great.

The Canon stayed outside the main stream of Irish politics but at the same time exerted a great influence through his writing in the journals of the day and also through his friends such as William O'Brien MP. The latter wrote of him as follows:

The Canon's work was that of a patriot, not of a politician. He was one of the few far-seeing Irishmen who realised all the possibilities of the Policy of Conciliation, inaugurated in 1902 under the Chief Secretaryship of Mr. George Wyndham. The first notable achievement of that policy was the Land Conference composed of the joint representatives of the landlords and tenants whose report was the basis of the great Land-purchase Act of 1903. By this measure the ownership of three-fourths of the soil of Ireland was transferred peacefully from the landlords to the cultivators by means of temporary annual payments. The transaction was effected by advances from the Imperial Treasury. The evicted tenants were, under the same agreement, restored to their holdings.

Those who had solved the agrarian difficulty proposed to proceed to the crowning settlement of the Home Rule problem by a similar method of Conference, Conciliation and Consent.

Although William O'Brien's comments may be true in substance, it is extremely doubtful if the Land Acts would have come into operation when they did without the impetus of the Land League where men like Davitt and Parnell led an agrarian movement, a movement in which many of its members including clergy suffered imprisonment to force the British Government into taking action.

Canon Sheehan did not belong to the Land League but the part he played in bringing to fruition the land transfers in Doneraile has been documented in an earlier chapter of this book. He never favoured a narrow nationalism and saw that a nationalist movement which was invariably Catholic orientated would eventually divide the country and in this he was right. His observations in the Cork Free Press in 1910 are worth noting.

We are a generous people and yet we are told that we must keep up sectarian bitterness to the end; and that Protestant Ascendancy has been broken down, only to build a Catholic Ascendancy on its ruins. Are we in earnest about out country at all, or are we seeking to perpetuate our wretchedness and backwardness by refusing honest aid of Irishmen ... It is from the Protestant minority that every great Irish leader for 150 years, except O'Connell, has sprung. It is that minority which has given us our greatest orators, our greatest statesmen, our leading merchants, our greatest archeologists, our first linguists, many of our greatest poets ... No power on earth can persuade us that a class which has given us such prodigies of genius as the first half of the nineteenth century did - genius too always devoted to the cause of Ireland - has been smitten with sudden barrenness.

The wide canvas of Canon Sheehan's nationalism through his writing was used to foster his ideas especially in the Cork Free Press. After some time however, his literary contributions to that paper ceased. In an article which appeared in the Caupuchin Annual entitled "My earliest Irish Friends". Mrs. Wm. O'Brien its author observed that her husband William "was grieved to hear from his friend (Canon Sheehan) that he had ceased his literary contributions (to the Cork Free Press). He did not explain the reason, a painful one. No more was said on the subject."

Canon Sheehan was the truest of Irishmen, a man who through his wide vision and true Christianity was always much more critical of the system which kept the Irish people down than of the individual. The thread of nationalism was woven through his writings, widening as he grew in years and in literary stature. As a boy he grew up in the Fenian tradition and about this he wrote with great sympathy and understanding.

Maynooth during his student days and for long afterwards was a very conservative seminary. At a concert there in 1879 he must have caused a stir when he recited 'The Year of Revolution'. As he himself described later:

The government of the House at that time was distinctly conservative if not anti-national; and it was certainly rash for a young student to select such a fierce, revolutionary ode for recitation in a college where there was a traditional dread of such things.

The enormous literary output of Canon Sheehan covered a very wide field but it was from his novels that his reputation was made. They can be classified under a number of headings. Those dealing with clerical life were My New Curate, Luke Delmege and The Blindness Of

Dr. Gray.   Those covering the social and political scene of rural Ireland were *Glenanaar, Lisheen, Miriam Lucas* and *The Graves at Kilmorna.* He wrote one historical novel *The Queen's Fillet* with the French Revolution as its theme and his first two books *Geoffrey Austin, Student* and *The Triumph Of Failure* dealt with student life. His book of short stories was called *A Spoiled Priest and other Stories.* Much of what he wrote in his early years was in the form of essays and articles and while, as was stated earlier, a number of them were intended to attract the attention of a clerical readership the response was not great and so he set out to use the novel as a platform to convey in a more subtle way the Gospel message. In this he was successful despite the fact that he drew down on him the wrath of critics, many of them his own clergy. He saw that with the improvement in social conditions and the power of the landlords waning, together with the advances being made towards Home Rule, a new Ireland was emerging and the Church's position would be challenged. Many priests, in his opinion, were oblivious to the dangers as he saw them and this he sought to highlight in his articles and books.

In the early decades of this century, there were few homes especially in rural Ireland where some or all of Canon Sheehan's books could not be found. Today he is a forgotten author except perhaps in the North Cork area of Doneraile, Mallow etc. A sad but yet a true statistic and well we may ask what kind of writer was this man whose books in the main lie now in obscurity. A small trickle of demand from the libraries for some of his books is about the only remnant of this man's literary fame to have survived.

Looking at the Irish sales figures of his books in the first few decades of the century and taking into account the fact that his books cost around six shillings (a half week's wages at least for a working man), he would be in the best seller list today for many of his books, if one were to go by the sales figures.

Although Canon Sheehan suffered at the hands of his literary critics while alive, much was written on his work in the decades after his death by friends and admirers. A great deal of it was honest comment but there was also a considerable amount of fulsome praise with little or no attempt whatsoever being made at a balanced appraisal of his work.

One often reads of Tolstoy's comment with reference to Canon Sheehan as "the greatest living writer". An exaggeration of course, if it ever had been made. Canon Sheehan was a good novelist of his time, but not a great one. A problem already referred to being his crisis of identity between priest and author and because of this his writing suffered. However, in fairness he did not set out to be a novelist. He did not really write to entertain, that was secondary to his primary motive which was to use the novel as a vehicle by which he got his Christian messages across both to clergy and laity. A close study of his books reveals that and the reader can clearly see the didactic way that many of them have been written. This detracted from them somewhat as novels, many of which were extremely popular and successful in that they followed the idea of the writer Robert Louis Stevenson that "the most influential books and the truest in their influence are works of fiction."

Most of Canon Sheehan's books were contrasted with *"My New Curate"* which was a great pity. Books such as *Luke Delmege, Glenanaar, The Blindness of Dr. Gray* were fine books in their own right. Yet, his priestly characters were always judged against 'Daddy Dan', the lovable old parish priest in *'My New Curate'*. As well as being inhibited as a novelist by his priestly calling, his writing possibly suffered also from the fact that he relied too much on the advice of others before going public with much of his writing. A case in point was Fr. Matthew Russell S.J., the Canon's literary confidant whose opinion he invariably sought out before going public with his books. This is no reflection on Fr. Russell's integrity but a writer if he is to be really true to his craft must express himself in a way that he himself thinks best.

Canon Sheehan's books nevertheless were written with a great depth of honesty and feeling. There was much of himself in many of his novels and his very forceful view that a sound moral teaching as a prerequisite for all intellectual teaching and study was well portrayed in his first two books, *Geoffrey Austin, Student,* and *The Triumph Of Failure.*

Because of the fact that he never mixed with other writers and there is little evidence to show that he even corresponded with many of them was somewhat of a disadvantage to him. He didn't create stage-Irish characters as many of his fellow scribes did but a weakness in his writing was his poor characterisation. Few of his characters created a lasting impression on the reader. True, there were many flashes of great characterisation such as the chapel woman in her confrontation with the curate Fr. Letheby in "My New Curate", but these were all too brief.

A friend of the Canon's Mr. D. L. Kelleher has left us with some interesting information about him as a writer. On a visit to Doneraile a year before the priest's death his host told him that he was not a methodical writer.

> Sometimes my brain lies fallow. then perhaps after a walk I
> return with my mind all activity again. Then I work for a
> while, often at two or three subjects on the same day

He told his friend that the Abbey Theatre movement interested him but regretted the negative attitude of its writers such as Synge and Yeats towards Christianity. He would have liked he said to meet the playwrite T. C. Murray.

"I suppose" said Mr. Kelleher, "you have people calling a great deal on you who have been attracted by your books?"

He laughed in reply saying "I used to be a curiosity. Americans often came to have a look at me - but now I am out of fashion."

It was sad that he felt the loneliness and of course the isolation. In his later years he travelled little. Perhaps to Cork twice in the year "and then I might walk Patrick Street without meeting one I knew".

An interesting fact in the evaluation of Canon Sheehan as a writer is that despite an international reputation he didn't warrant a mention in Daniel Corkery's *Synge and Anglo Irish Literature*. It was a sad reflection on a writer of Sheehan's standing. The Canon was not in Corkery's mould of nationalism, which was very much of the Republican tradition. Sheehan's nationalism was much broader than that. There is no doubt but it was a deliberate snub to Canon Sheehan when one reads the criteria which Corkery laid down to be an Irish writer.

He maintained that a real national Irish literature could never come from the pen of any anglo-Irish writer. It could only come from a true

Irish person who would have absorbed and understood (a) the religious consciousness of the people; (b) the Land Question and (c) Irish Nationalism.

No one was better fitted to match Corkery's criteria than Canon Sheehan, yet he chose to ignore him. As a priest, who better to have absorbed and understood the religious consciousness of the Irish people. He had worked among them long enough. Although as already stated, he was not involved directly with the Land League he did however play a major part in assisting the tenant farmers. His nationalism has already been referred to.

It is important when looking at the writings of Canon Sheehan to assess them in the context that they were written eighty years ago or more and that our criticisms are being made with the benefit of that period of hindsight. However, having said that there are flaws in his novels which may account to some extent for the loss of their appeal in to-day's world.

Many of his books were long and drawn out, tending to preach somewhat to readers. Characterisation outside of his priestly characters was not great as for example those of the gentry. His priests were very human indeed and he showed their flaws as well as their good points. He was criticised too for the many quotations and phrases he used in his books, it being looked upon as rather show-offish. In reality of course, he was in no way like that.

Many of Canon Sheehan's books would be looked on as rather old fashioned today. Much of his writing made sad reading in that it showed very little light at the end of the tunnel for Ireland. Some of the novels showed very little hope and offered no great solutions for his country's problems.

On close inspection, the ordinary people characterised in his novels were not portrayed as being of the brightest. Mostly they came across as rather dull and dim witted, and not people one could look to in the shaping of new Ireland. Back in 1900, Fr. Matthew Russell, S.J. said in a letter to the Canon that Dr. Brendan McCarthy, a son of the poet Denis Florence McCarthy had made a similar observation:

> "Dr. McCarthy thinks you run down our poor people too much".

and in fact Fr. Russell himself once said:

I object to the idea that Canon Sheehan gives of our Irish people. It is not like the people at all as I have seen them.

Very few of those portrayed actually appeared to have a job of any responsibility and if unsupervised, they would surely drift away to other pursuits. The fact that he did not deal in any depth with the agrarian problems of the country and the social conditions under which people lived were marks against him. Little resentment appeared to come from the characters he created towards their conditions. They were portrayed as being happy enough with their lot and with their station in life.

Socialism and the development of the labour movement was also not adequately dealt with in Canon Sheehan's novels and the activities of the Land League, supported in very many cases by the clergy were similarly neglected. Yet despite all the flaws his books were a major force in Irish writing at the turn of the century and for many years afterwards.

The sales figures available for most of the Canon's books in Ireland make interesting reading. Sales of his first book *Geoffrey Austin, Student* amounted to 3200 copies. The figures from the Longmans publishing group (Messrs Longmans Green & Co. in Canon Sheehan's time) who published most of his books are as follows:

The Blindness Of Dr. Gray (18,400); Early Essays & Lectures (2,500); Glenanaar (11,700); The Graves at Kilmorna (13,000); The Intellectuals (imported from New York - 1600); *Lisheen (11,600); Lost Angel of a Ruined Paradise (3,500); Luke Delmege (12,000); Miriam Lucas (11,300); My New Curate* (Stock received since 1928 - 2,800), *Parerga* (imported from New York - 1,800); *The Queen's Fillet - (11,500); Tristram Lloyd* (stock received since 1929 - 900).

It is to be noted that Longman's were not the publishers of Canon Sheehan's most famous book, *My New Curate*. It was published by

Marlier & Co. in New York. Over 30,000 copies were sold in Ireland in the first 18 months. American sales and those by the Talbot Press are not quoted. There were very large sales of Canon Sheehan's other books also in America and of course in Europe where he was translated into many languages as for example *My New Curate* which was translated into German, French, Spanish, Dutch, Italian, Hungarian, Slavonic and Russian. *Under the Cedars and the Stars* was published in America. These are very impressive sales figures and compare favourably with the sales of many books published in Ireland today.

Sales figures for Canon Sheehan's books translated into Irish up to early 1940 were as follows:

Gleann an Air (2099); *Lisin* (1500); *Filead na Bannrioghna* (110); *An Sagart Og* (1175).

In 1909, the *Irish Monthly* in its April edition published the text of a lecture given by Canon Sheehan to the Cork Literary and Scientific Society. It told much of the role of the writer in society at that time and answered the many questions put to authors. He didn't raise the hopes and aspirations of many would - be writers in his audience when early on in his talk he quoted the lines of Dr. Johnson:

> You know what ills the author's life assail
> Toil, envy, want, the patron and the jail.

True, he said, there were those who made money, real money such as Lord Macauley who got £10,000 for his History of England, a princely sum in the middle of the 1800s and Dickens who on his death bed left behind six times that amount. But there were many writers, the majority in fact who found it impossible to make a living from their craft. What of Milton, he asked, who got five pounds for *Paradise Lost*. There was Goldsmith, Jane Austin etc. whose rewards were meagre. Canon Sheehan was more successful than many writers of his period and his writings earned him a considerable income much of which went to charitable causes in the diocese of Cloyne.

In his lecture he posed the question as to why did people take up their pens and go through the process of not alone spending months, even years on some work only to have it rejected on publication but also suffering the tirades of abuse and criticism that such a venture entailed. The answers he said could be summed up in:

> Admiration for great authors and the desire to imitate them; a passionate love for books and the ambition to create something similar; the craving for what is believed to be a quiet, uneventful, unimpassioned life; the fancy that a life of literature is absolutely free from care; the rapture of composition; the desire of fame; the passion, so universal, for making money as speedily and as easily as possible.

He himself felt that in many ways a literary life was for the most part an unhappy one because if you had talent, there were so many cares and worries 'incidental to the circumstances of men of letters as to make life exceedingly miserable.' He pointed out too that it was difficult to convince a young author that publishers didn't always publish their best work, they were business men engaged in profit and loss where often popularity of a certain item superseded the high literary quality of a not so popular subject and went on to say:

> But supposing your book fairly launched, its perils are only beginning. You have to run the gauntlet of the critics. To a young author, again, this seems to be as terrible an ordeal as passing down the files of Sioux or Comanche Indians, each one of whom is thirsting for your scalp. When you are a little older, you will find that criticism is not much more serious than the by-play of clowns in a circus when they beat around the ring the victim with bladders slung at the end of long-poles. A time comes in the life of every author when he regards critics as comical, rather than formidable and goes his way unheeding. But there are sensitive souls that yield under the chastisement and perhaps, after suffering much silent torture, abandon the profession of the pen forever.

Canon Sheehan himself felt the critic's rapier on many occasions. He was deeply sensitive about it in his early writing years. Later he was able to come to terms with it but never fully mastered it. Despite all the ups and downs and there were many 'downs', he said to those whose tastes lead in a literary direction, he recommended it for three reasons - as a source of pleasure and enjoyment for one's self; as a refining and exalting influence and thirdly as a possible apostolate.

Despite being an extremely popular writer in his day, we must pose the question as to why did his books fade into oblivion. Apart from the many aspects already discussed, there was the fact that in the decade following his death Ireland underwent enormous political and social change. The 1916 rebellion and the Civil War caused profound changes throughout the country. Sheehan's broad nationalism and deferences to his Church had to a great extent been turned upside down and the novels through which he endeavoured to propound his ideas lost their appeal.

Canon Sheehan was an enigmatic writer and appeared to be more nationalistic when portraying events that were not of the times in which he lived as a priest such as those of the Fenians while the Land War and its effects on the rural community and the upsurge of socialism which were of his time were not brought to life as they should have been in his novels. Here as the priest, he was in a dilemma and tried to steer a centre course.

As mentioned earlier the didactic nature of his books did not find favour with the Irish people when they became more educated and better informed and so they changed their allegiance to other writers. The Irish Revival movement with Yeats and Lady Gregory on centre stage stole the show from the Doneraile P.P. Shaw too with his satirical writing drew the attention of many.

The advent of radio and later television has done little or nothing to popularise the books of Canon Sheehan. The works of many writers of the past have had a new life through their serialisation but those of Sheehan have been neglected. Some of his books would make good TV viewing and would be a social document on Ireland in the last century. *My New Curate* and *The Blindness of Dr. Gray* would lend themselves to serialisation as most certainly would *Glenaaar* with its powerful theme of the Doneraile Conspiracy.

Canon Sheehan was a man who through his great scholarship enunciated the voice of rural Ireland in the 19th century and his books mirrored that period. They were written with the greatest of integrity, an integrity which often caused him great suffering due to the harshness of his critics. And while his novels became the victim of the difficult choice between Priest and author, nevertheless many of them were really fine works written in a true Christian spirit and do not warrant the neglect that they now endure. Sadly, Canon Sheehan as an author is much forgotten but the high moral values and integrity which were the soul of his writing are as necessary today as they were when he first began to write.

REFERENCES

Correspondence and documents re Canon Sheehan from the papers of Herman J. Heuser, D.D., (1872-1933) in the archives of St. Charles Borromeo Seminary, Overbrook, Philadelphia, USA.

The Holmes-Sheehan correspondence (1903-1913) - National University Publications, Port Washington, New York and from the Heuser Papers.

Canon Sheehan of Doneraile - Herman J. Heuser D.D. (1917).

Canon Sheehan: A Sketch of his Life and Works - Rev. F. Boyle (1927).

Canon Sheehan of Doneraile - M.P. Linehan (1952).

Essays in Irish Biography - Canon Sheehan and his People.

Canon Sheehan of Doneraile - Kenneth MacGowan (Catholic Truth Society Publication).

Canon Sheehan - Rev. Ml. J. Phelan, S.J. (Catholic Truth Society Publication).

A History of Doneraile - Fr. A. Gaughan.

A History of Mallow - Sister E. Bolster.

The Capuchin Annuals.

The Works of Canon Sheehan.

The following publications: The Irish Ecclesiastical Record; The American Ecclesiastical Review; Irish Writing; Studies; The New Ireland Review; The Bell; The Irish Monthly; The Christian Brothers Educational Record; St. Stephen's Magazine; The Catholic Bulletin; The Catholic Truth Society; Irish Book Lover; Seanchas Duthalla; The Mallow Field Club Journals; The Pioneer; The Dublin Magazine; The Messenger; Journals of the Cork Historical & Archeological Society; The Dublin Review.

The Doneraile Conspiracy - Articles by Michael Shine ("Corkman" 1988).

The Churches of Doneraile - Article by Michael Shine (Mallow Field Club Journal 1989).

Devotional Revolutional in Ireland 1850-1875 - Emmet Larkin (1972).

Paul Cardinal Cullen - Desmond Bowen (1983).

Articles - The Making of the Roman Catholic Church In Ireland 1850-1860 - Emmet Larkin.

Interviews re Canon Sheehan broadcast RTE 2nd October 1988.

The National and Provincial Press.

Also referred to were the following:

Thesis on Canon Sheehan - T. J. MacElligott, M.A. (1942):
Thesis - Twentieth Century Rural Ireland in Novels by Canon Sheehan, Brisnley MacNamara and Patk. Kavanagh - Ruth Fleischmann (1983)

Lectures and discussions re the works of Canon Sheehan delivered at various North Cork Writers' Festivals in Doneraile by J.P. Lovett, M.A., Dr. Colbert Kearney, Miss Ruth Fleischmann and the late Padraig O Maidin;

Synge and Anglo-Irish Literature - Daniel Corkery;
Fireside Hours - William O'Brien

Letters from Canon Sheehan to Fr. Russell, S.J. as published and commented on by Rev. Fr. Robert Forde in Seanchas Duthalla (1979-1980) and in the Mallow Field Club Journal (1986).

Reminiscences of Canon Sheehan and interviews.

INDEX